Contents

Foreword   v

Acknowledgments   ix

Introduction   xiii

Chapter 1

Set Expectations to Avoid Performance Issues   1

Chapter 2

The Four-Step Model to Getting Performance Management
Right Every Time: Start Where You Are   21

Chapter 3

Communicate Clearly and Often   39

Chapter 4

Accelerate Performance Success: From 0 to 60 in
Real Situations   67

Chapter 5

How Leaders Can Be Proactive (and Not Reactive) with
Performance: Make a Plan and Follow It   107

Chapter 6

30 Starters for Tough Performance Conversations: Waiting
and Hoping Won't Cut It   121

Chapter 7

Managing Performance in Today's Dynamic Workplace   155

Chapter 8

Coach and Develop: Case Studies, Templates, and Tools   169

Chapter 9

Measuring Performance to Spot Problems Early   203

Chapter 10

Using the Strategies Successfully in Your Organization   229

Index   247

Foreword

I have been in the human resources profession for going on 20 years, and I can finally say that I have found in this book, *Solving Employee Performance Problems: How to Spot Problems Early, Take Appropriate Action, and Bring Out the Best in Everyone,* an invaluable resource that I am using almost daily, primarily because this is a book that delivers on its title's promise.

I have found this book to be a practical road map and compass— a navigational tool that can help guide almost any leader, HR professional, manager, supervisor, or business owner, along with his or her organization, closer to reaching *best-in-class* status. Just like you, at every conference, professional meeting, convention, and book signing event I attend, I've been looking for a resource that will enhance employee performance and take my organization to the next level. Additionally, I look for resources that show me new, creative ways to handle specific performance problems when they arise, offer positive solutions and nonambiguous statements when called for, stop the guessing game of hunting for the perfect verbiage, and whenever possible, just make my life easier by saving me time and eliminating the frustration of trying to spin all the plates of constructive and caring discipline in the workplace.

At its core, this book resonates with the critical importance of treating employees with dignity and respect, honoring everyone's unique differences, and motivating and developing employees and their competencies to a higher plane of performance. Isn't that what we all seek to achieve in our organizations? This approach is clearly demonstrated throughout this book with easy-to-use toolkits and templates you'll refer to regularly, including mini and real-world case studies, dozens of tough performance conversation starters, employee coaching and development forms, and timely techniques that you can pull right out of this book and use on the spot—just-in-time solutions to real-world employee performance problems when you need them most.

Inevitably employee problems and a wide variety of people challenges are going to surface in the workplace for all of us, no matter how happy or successful our corporate culture might be. The creative bent to this book is that it not only "reads our minds" on what we've all been thinking and wanting to address better, but it gives us as readers specific ways we can address the most difficult employee issues, including drama in the workplace, tardiness, insubordination, abuse of Family and Medical Leave Act (FMLA) regulations, profanity, and so on, and then provides concrete ways to build a framework for structuring solutions in partnership with employees.

Clearly when we all learn to confront performance issues head on and more effectively, we also learn to better build our organization's employee brand, we increase confidence among the workforce, we create ongoing employee/employer loyalty, and we garner inspired buy-in and team building. It's a win-win for everybody. It's ROI at its best—return on investment in people and return on integrity of the organization!

As leaders we have to keep attracting top talent—we can never let up—and then we must encourage that talent to be its best and keep reaching higher goals that take that talent to the next level. That requires each of us as a leader to be fair and equitable, compassionate, and true to ourselves.

This book helps do that with decorum and grace. It takes a forward-thinking approach to an often backward-thinking strategy on progressive disciplinary actions and employee performance problem solving. You'll not find here yesterday's outdated HR methods for mandating employee job performance and compliance. Instead, you'll find a refreshing approach to inspiring innovation on the job, stronger people skills–building techniques, and methods for growing talent for maximizing individual strengths.

As an HR professional and organizational leader in one of the most admired and desirable companies to work for in California, I have been looking for a book like this for a long time. I am recommending it to my colleagues and have my entire HR team reading it now as a professional development project.

This book reminds us that human resources is both a head and heart issue. With our acknowledgment and increasing value of human capital in the workplace, technologies that have changed and will continue to change us all at breakneck speed, as well as globalization and the core requirements that company leaders and employees must learn to better communicate and interact with one another, an entire new world of performance challenges and HR issues has surfaced.

With the help of this book as a go-to resource, I plan to ready myself with the mastery of technical, professional, and people-oriented competencies that require head and heart, business acumen, emotional intelligence, and tangible contributions to my HR community and to the organization and the people I serve.

Stephanie Montanez
Director of Human Resources
MedAmerica Billing Services, Inc.
and member of the Society for
Human Resources Management (PHR) and
the National Human Resources Association

Acknowledgments

Brenda Hampel

It has truly been an honor to be a coauthor on this book with Anne Bruce and Erika Lamont. Anne gave Erika and me the opportunity to partner with her as we ventured into the publishing world. Her expertise, motivation, professionalism, and friendship have made our participation and this book a reality.

Thank you to my business partner and closest friend Erika Lamont. She constantly gives me perspective, support, and most importantly the opportunity to do the work that I love with a person who makes the work fun and fulfilling.

My inspiration and knowledge base for this book comes from my background as a human resources professional. I have been very fortunate to have both roles and bosses that gave me the opportunity to learn, make mistakes, and build confidence to manage and support leaders. The most important message that I heard was that the purpose of human resources is to support the business—so learn the business. Taking this to heart allowed me to gain credibility and serve as a true business partner to leaders. My job was (and is) to help leaders become better leaders to their team and the organization as a whole.

A special note of appreciation goes to my wonderful friend Wendy Schutt. Her attention to detail, focus, and fantastic organization skills helped me put order to this book. Her awesome supplies and sense of humor make the detail work fun!

I am grateful for the clients that I have the privilege of working with—they allow me to apply the skills and strategies outlined in this book, and they continue to stretch me as a professional. I am very fortunate to do work with people who inspire me.

Most important I want to thank my husband Jeff and our daughters Alex and Jordan. My family gives me the support, encouragement, and flexibility to do my work. Jeff is my confidante, sounding board, and advisor. He always tells me, "You can!"

Erika Lamont

The collaboration on this project with Brenda Hampel and Anne Bruce has undoubtedly produced tears of laughter, pride, frustration, relief, and joy. We have worked hard and laughed harder while writing, rewriting, e-mailing, editing, and reading, and we are now looking forward to seeing the "reward" of success stories that result from leaders in organizations employing the strategies that are outlined in this book. We have seen firsthand the power of these conversations and know that they will work for your organization and your employees.

My close friend and business partner, Brenda, knows how to do this stuff in her sleep, and it is largely her knowledge, experience, and wisdom that are contained here. I have been telling her for years that we just need to get it out of her brain and into a book! She is my inspiration and motivation, and I appreciate her every day.

Anne has been our guide and cheerleader. Her mentorship and friendship have been invaluable, and I thank her for that. I also want to thank my family for their love and support, my husband Michael, who told me that, yes, in fact I could write a book, and last, my daughters Elizabeth and Maggie, for frequently "reminding" me of my deadlines.

Anne Bruce

Eighteen years ago, while I was delivering a keynote speech in Dallas for the American Management Association, I was greeted by a man with a business card as I came off the speaker platform. He was an editor for McGraw-Hill Publishing in New York. He handed me his card and said, "Can you write as well as you speak?" It was that fateful encounter that launched a longtime relationship with my publisher and many good friends and wonderful people at McGraw-Hill. This is my fifteenth book, and I'm happy to be back working with a super fantastic editor and friend Mary Glenn. And with this new book, I have had the pleasure to meet and work with, for the first time, senior editor Knox Huston. Knox, you've been great to work with on every level of this project. Your unflappable sense of humor has kept me plowing through those deadlines. Thanks to everyone at McGraw-Hill who is working on this book, including Jane Palmieri, editing manager, and Roberta Mantus, copyeditor, not to mention an amazing art department for a great cover and numerous illustrations. You all rock!

I have learned over the years that it is often the serendipitous or seemingly random events in life that can drastically alter and change the trajectory of things. Such a pivotal moment happened for me when I was introduced by my good friends and fellow authors Lawrence Polsky and Antoine Gerschel to my two writing partners Brenda Hampel and Erika Lamont. Thank you Brenda and Erika for generously providing your creative ideas, nonstop enthusiasm, and sisterlike friendship to this project. Partnering with you both on this book has been both an honor and a blast. You both lifted my spirits greatly when I was schlepping boxes of books through airport after airport while on the road, and you both made me laugh out loud when my hotel room was the target of a bee invasion in Tucson! I admire your brilliance, success, and genuine way of making all those around you feel a bit smarter and better for having known you. I am one of those people.

In addition, this book would not have been possible without the generous ongoing contributions, ideas, research, contacts, and never-ending sparks of enormous wisdom and inspiration from HR experts and special friends and colleagues, like Stephanie Montanez and Courtney Proffitt; publicity and marketing consultant at SpiritusCommunications.com, the amazing Jocelyn Godfrey; AnneBruce.com Web site fashionista and dear friend Elly Mixsell; and superstar copyeditor and oh-so-dependable friend and colleague Phyllis Salamone Jask.

Thank you to every person who has ever attended one of my keynote speeches or training programs and to all of you who keep coming back, buying more books, and telling others about my work. You all continue to enrich my life by allowing me to be a part of yours.

Finally, I extend my deepest love and gratitude to my husband David and my daughter Autumn for always loving me, inspiring me, and lifting me to new, exciting, and unpredictable heights. Whenever opportunity knocks, you are both there cheering me on and gently pushing me through the doorway. You give my life more meaning and purpose than you will ever know.

Introduction

Why is it so difficult for most of us (leaders) to have timely and productive performance conversations? There are lots of reasons—none of them valid.

Leaders tell us that the reasons they don't have or procrastinate having performance conversations are:

- It is so obvious that the employee must know and should be correcting the problem.
- I don't have time.
- I tried, and nothing changed.
- I'm not sure what I can and cannot say—my HR rep warns me about lawsuits.
- I've never had or am uncomfortable with this type of conversation—I'm not sure where or how to start.

Our responses are:

- These situations are rarely clear to the employee. It is not realistic to expect that employees will make changes they do not know they should make.
- You are more than likely spending more time dealing with the consequences of the performance issue than it would take to have a productive performance conversation.
- Many leaders believe they have performance conversations and are frustrated with the lack of "responsiveness" from the employees. Most of the time employees do not recall having a performance conversation and are unaware of any problems.
- It is important to understand the dos and don'ts of performance conversations. However, once you understand how to prepare for and have these conversations, you will stay on the right course.
- Don't worry—by applying the tools and resources included in this book, you will become skilled at having successful performance conversations.

Now that we have addressed the reasons and excuses for not having successful performance conversations, let's see how best-in-class organizations and leaders have performance conversations.

A recent report published by the Aberdeen Group surfaced the primary themes that drive performance management.

The report validated the clear tie between managing performance and business operations. Companies that achieve best-in-class results in employee performance management are those in which employees are engaged in the work, where individuals are meeting and exceeding individual performance goals, and where employees are able to best serve the needs of the customer. The key to creating this type of work environment lies with the business leaders. The top five capabilities put in place by these top-performing companies all have to do with the manager's role in helping to draw links between individuals and the growth goals of the organization:

1. Managers meet with employees on a regular basis.
2. Managers are held accountable for managing performance.
3. The performance management process enables leaders to assign individual goals that are linked to organizational goals.
4. Managers are held accountable for employees attaining their goals.
5. Leaders are trained to execute performance management strategy.

Best-in-class organizations state that the top two barriers to effective performance management are lack of follow-up between leaders and employees regarding progress toward goals and performance expectations followed by difficulty communicating the organization's strategy. It was found that these managers rely too heavily on a manual process for communicating with employees, while managers in best-in-class organizations use technology, such as the company intranet, and regularly scheduled staff and one-on-one meetings that consistently include an agenda item to communicate to provide updates on performance and the strategic plan. Obviously these leaders are not having performance conversations with their team members. The lack of interaction has a negative impact on business results. In addition, leaders who are not managing the performance of their team members are leaving a gap in developing organizational talent. When leaders demonstrate through their actions that they take their responsibility seriously, they become a model for the managers on their team.

This book provides leaders with examples and templates that will enable them to have performance conversations that will allow them to contribute to the organization's objectives and talent development.

Let's back up and look at the big picture before we take a deeper dive into the why, how, and when of having performance conversations.

The following graphic outlines the talent management cycle, which reminds us of the different stages employees go through. Without productive, performance conversations, employees cannot effectively move through each of these stages. And the organization does

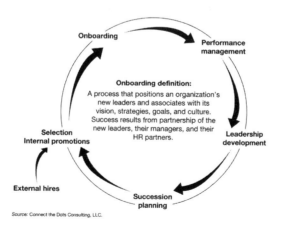

Source: Connect the Dots Consulting, LLC.

not see a return on the investment made in each employee. Instead the employees "stumble" to and through each phase without clearly understanding how they are doing, and they have no reason to make changes needed to have a positive impact.

What happens both during and in between each of these stages that "causes" these performance issues in the first place? The answer typically comes down to the level of communication between the leader and the employee. Do leaders understand that a significant part of their role is to set their team members up for success? Do they have the communication and coaching skills to spend most of their time proactively managing performance and effectively handling performance challenges that surface? Most leaders struggle with communication and coaching; many were promoted because of their strong technical or operational performance and are expected to suddenly develop leadership skills. Of course this is setting the leader up for failure or at best "spotty" success. This book is designed to provide leaders and human resources partners with resources, talking points, and strategies to build and implement the skills needed to be leaders that proactively manage their teams' performance through effective communication and coaching. It is often a difficult road with lots of mistakes made along the way; it should be viewed as a marathon and not a sprint. The payoff comes when the leader has a high-functioning team whose members have a clear understanding of what they are being held accountable for. With such a team, performance issues are handled efficiently and professionally.

To cross the finish line, leaders must make a commitment, look for opportunities to practice, get feedback on how they are doing, make adjustments, and practice again.

The 10 chapters that follow can be used as standalone resources to support you as you address specific performance challenges. They will provide you with a clear understanding of how to build your performance management skills.

Make the commitment and enjoy the journey.

Solving Employee Performance Problems

How to Spot Problems Early, Take Appropriate Action, and .... veryone

Anne Br...

Brenda H...

Erika La...

New York .... rid   Mexico City

Milan .... ey   Toronto

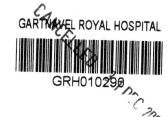

1 2 3 4 5 6 7 8 9 10   QFR/QFR   1 9 8 7 6 5 4 3 2 1

ISBN   978-0-07-176907-5

MHID   0-07-176907-2

e-ISBN   978-0-07-176991-4

e-MHID 0-07-176991-9

Library of Congress Cataloging-in-Publication Data

Bruce, Anne

Solving employee performance problems : how to spot problems early, take appropriate action, and bring out the best in everyone / by Anne Bruce, Brenda Hampel, and Erika Lamont.

p. cm.

Includes index.

ISBN 978-0-07-176907-5 (alk. paper)

1. Performance standards. 2. Employees—Rating of. 3. Problem employees— Rating of. I. Hampel, Brenda. II. Lamont, Erika. III. Title.

HF5549.5.P35B78 2011

658.3'128—dc22

2011008759

McGraw-Hill books are available at special quantity discounts to use as premiums and sales promotions or for use in corporate training programs. To contact a representative, please e-mail us at bulksales@mcgraw-hill.com.

This book is printed on acid-free paper.

Chapter 1

Set Expectations to Avoid Performance Issues

"An ounce of prevention is worth a pound of cure."

As our research and our work has told us, many performance issues result from the lack of understanding of performance expectations or the lack of clarity of those expectations. Without a clear target, it is impossible for employees to know where and for what to aim. On the flip side, their managers should not be able to hold them accountable without these same measures or tools.

Leaders need to build a performance-based team whose objectives are consistent with the organization's vision and mission.

CREATING TEAMS

The synergy that comes from putting employees together to form teams to solve problems, make decisions, and take action is power that organizations can harness for greater success. In these increasingly complex, changing times for your business, using the principles of teams can supply more creative solutions and more powerful support for your teams and the organization as a whole. With an effective team, "The whole is greater than the sum of its parts."

Creating teams and leading them to success require skill and finesse on the part of the team leaders. We discuss and provide practice for the skills that can help make you successful in creating a good team environment.

> *Teamwork* is the ability of people to work together toward a common vision. It is the ability to direct individual accomplishment toward organizational objectives, and it is the fuel that allows common people to attain uncommon results.

WHAT DOES A TEAM LOOK LIKE?

To help you determine whether you have a team or just a group of individuals, consider the following questions:

- How do you make decisions?
- How do you deal with conflicts?
- How do you solve problems?
- What happens when things go wrong?
- How do you build a team that makes effective decisions, surfaces and manages conflicts, and works together to solve problems and handle issues?

BUILDING THE VISION

At the center of every high-performance team is a common purpose, a mission that rises above and beyond each of the individual team members. To be successful, the team's interests and needs must come first. This requires, "we-opic" vision ("What's in it for 'we'?"). A challenging step up from the common, "me-opic" mindset.

To embrace this principle, make sure your team purpose and priorities are clear. What is your overall mission? What is your game plan? What is expected of each team member? How can each member contribute most effectively? What constants will hold the team together? Then stop and ask yourself whether you are putting the team first.

In order to develop successful plans, it is necessary for managers both to understand their organization's strategic vision and to incorporate that vision into their plans and day-to-day operations. To accomplish this, consider the following steps:

1. Become comfortable articulating your organization's vision and strategic direction. To clarify and increase your understanding in this area, ask yourself questions such as:

   ☐ What is the organization's strategic vision?
   ☐ What does the strategic vision mean for me and my department?
   ☐ What are the future opportunities?
   ☐ What talents and resources will I need to accomplish my part?

2. Ask for whatever information you need to understand the strategy and direction.

3. Link your operational plans with the organization's vision and strategic direction.

4. Plan for ongoing review and updates to ensure that your departmental plans support your organization's strategic vision.

Company's Vision/Strategy

Write your vision here:

_____

_____

_____

_____

_____

If you are unclear about your company's vision, you can get more information by:

- Reading the annual report.
- Attending company meetings, such as town meetings, and reading quarterly updates, newsletters, and press releases.
- Talking with members of the management team.
- Reviewing annual objectives.

Your Team's Vision

What is the vision for your current team? What is the purpose of the team? How does your vision fit into the company's overall vision and strategy?

Team Vision: Write your team vision here:
Purpose of Team: Write your team purpose here:
How Does the Team Vision Fit into the Company's Vision/Strategy?

MAKING THE VISION HAPPEN

Now that you have established your vision, established clear expectations for each team member, and assessed the strengths and weaknesses of your team, it is time to implement the vision and make it happen. The first step in making it happen is communicating the vision and keeping it alive. Use the following worksheet to develop your communication plan.

Team Vision			
Team Member	**Key Responsibilities**	**Skills and Abilities**	**Rewards**

COMMUNICATE, COMMUNICATE, COMMUNICATE

The communication process can also be thought of as a public relations initiative. As we learn in the case studies in Chapter 8, the team's purpose and vision not only needs to be communicated to the team members, but they also need to be communicated to the rest of the organization, particularly those functions with which the teams will be working closely.

STRATEGIES FOR COMMUNICATING WITH YOUR TEAM

Many leaders are focused on tasks, results, and projects. While these items are important, leaders must also take the time to communicate with their teams. Effectively communicating with team members increases productivity and minimizes confusion and wasted effort. The following strategies outline opportunities for leaders to communicate with their teams.

- Hold regular staff meetings:
  - ☐ Make these important meetings a priority.
  - ☐ Plan an agenda, allowing for changes when needed.
  - ☐ Include a development activity on a regular basis.
- Keep formal department documents up to date, such as:
  - ☐ Organizational charts
  - ☐ Department vision
  - ☐ Management by objectives (MBOs)
- Hold regular breakfast or lunch meetings monthly or quarterly:
  - ☐ Discuss current items affecting the department.
  - ☐ Cover broader items that are happening in the organization.
  - ☐ Allow for and encourage questions.
- Display current "news" items. Put up a bulletin board or something similar for department and company news items to be placed. Keep it current.
- Hold impromptu meetings as needed. When new, urgent information comes to your attention, share this information with those on your team who are affected.
- Return phone and e-mail messages to your team members promptly.
- Develop your own way of sending handwritten notes to your team members.

How to communicate with your manager:

- Have regularly scheduled meetings with your manager. If he or she does not initiate them, arrange to get on his or her calendar.
- Know how your manager prefers to receive information.
- Make sure there are no surprises:
  - Keep your manager informed of any important issues that affect your team.
  - Invite your manager periodically to attend your staff meetings.
- Make use of informal opportunities, such as lunches, travel, and social events to communicate with your manager.

STRATEGIES FOR COMMUNICATING WITH OTHER KEY GROUPS

In addition to effectively communicating inside the team, it is also critical that leaders develop strong communication across departments. Clear and open communication channels between departments have several advantages: surfaces issues, problem solving, minimizes rework, and increases productivity. Below is a list of strategies to first identify these key groups and then foster strong communication with them.

- Identify the key groups that your team needs to interact with.
- Develop relationships with your peers in those groups.
- Create opportunities to relay pertinent information on your team's activities and successes to these key groups. Opportunities might include:
  - Your manager's staff meetings
  - Newsletters
  - Lunches
  - Meetings that include members of these groups

The next step is to understand how to apply the strategies within your specific company culture.

> *Company culture* is made up of the psychology, attitudes, experiences, beliefs, and values (personal and cultural) of an organization. It has been defined as "the specific collection of values and norms that are shared by people and groups in an organization and that control the way they interact with each other and with stakeholders outside the organization."

UNDERSTANDING A COMPANY'S CULTURE

Answers to the following questions can help uncover and articulate a company culture:

1. How would you describe this company? Answer as if you were describing a person (three words). When you talk about where you work, what do you tell people?

2. What does the company value? What is important here? How do you know it's important?

3. What areas are dominant here? Does marketing lead, or finance, or production? Why?

4. What are the "unwritten rules" for getting along in this organization? What do we always do? Never do?

5. How does the organization handle conflict? Good news? Bad news? Deadlines? Decision making? (Provide examples of ways that the company has handled crises.)

6. Whom do you see as the primary customers of the company? What happens when a key customer complains? To what extent does the company hold true to its expressed standards for dealing with its customers? Shareholders? Stakeholders? Employees?

Having a clear understanding of the culture provides leaders with important context for managing performance situations. Without this context leaders are vulnerable to making mistakes and taking missteps that can lead to larger and potentially risky situations.

A leader's HR partner is typically a good resource for explaining the company culture as well as how performance is managed within the culture. Successful leaders join with their HR partners to gain an understanding of the culture and how to navigate within it.

ONBOARDING: A FRESH START

Starting a new role or hiring a new employee is one of the few opportunities that we have in our professional experiences to start with a clean state. It is critical to take advantage of this unique opportunity. This fresh start allows us either as the manager or as the new employee to set clear expectations or establish performance standards that in turn allow us to avoid many common performance problems. So how do we do this?

STEP ONE: START WITH A PLAN

After orientation, a new employee usually reports to his work area and hopefully is allowed to get acquainted with his coworkers, the physical environment, and his manager. This is a pretty easy process, and most new hires and their teams are excited to get to know one another and are looking for ways to make the transition smooth. There are times, however, when this initial excitement wears off quickly, and new hires are left to "figure things out" by themselves with no structure or plan. Managers who don't hire people often are usually the ones guilty of not putting enough thought and preparation into how their new hires will spend those first few days, weeks, and months on the job. The managers may start with great intentions and have a few early meetings, but then not give the new employee enough to do, or give him too much information to absorb at once. The manager, and the rest of the team, will quickly revert back to their work habits and routine, without much consideration of the new hire. Sometimes a coworker or "buddy" will be assigned to train or get the new employee up to speed. This can work effectively if the coworker is engaged and clearly understands what is expected during this process. Unfortunately, what typically happens is that the new hire shadows this person without a clear picture of how what he's seeing relates to his job. He feels like a burden because he cannot contribute much to the process. It is also common for the responsibility of new-hire training to fall on a select few individuals who can become quickly burned out because they are called upon too often to show the ropes to new people in their department.

The Critical Importance of an Onboarding Plan

What is missing from the typical scenario is an onboarding plan. Some refer to it as a 90-day plan or a transition or integration plan. Whatever you call it, the important thing is to have one! As soon as the job offer has been accepted by the candidate, the hiring manager, with the help of her HR partner, should discuss the most important things that this new hire must do during his first few months on the job.

Equally important is identifying the people with whom he needs to build relationships in order for him to accomplish those things. Just the concept of having a 90-day plan gives both the manager and the new hire the opportunity to use the first weeks as a chance to both "learn and do." It is important to have a healthy balance of getting and absorbing information and actually delivering work. Too often organizations are heavy on one or the other. Some expect new employees to sit in their offices or work spaces and read binders full of policies and procedures, or voluminous reports, or endless e-learning programs with no context. Others have demand for work and expect the new employee to hit the ground running and start to contribute immediately.

There are always various definitions of what exactly "immediately" means, and this creates unrealistic expectations both for the new hire and for the organization. The work delivered is often of low quality or just wrong, which results in rework and frustration from the new hire and the organization.

Building In Quick Hits and Early Wins

The onboarding plan takes into account both the *type* of information that a new hire needs and *when* he needs it. It also identifies "quick hits" or "early wins," which are those smaller objectives and tasks that new employees can accomplish and check off the list so that they feel like they are contributing to the business while gaining credibility and traction in their new role.

A good onboarding program lays out the specific roles and responsibilities of all the participants. We find that the best-practice onboarding programs use the "three-legged stool" model of onboarding. The hiring manager, the HR partner, and the new employee are all key participants in the process and have specific roles that are played out. If any one of the participants fails to perform his or her part of the process, one of the legs is "broken," and the onboarding experience is not as effective as it could be. We also find it extremely helpful to spell out the roles and responsibilities of each of these process participants as they are being introduced to the onboarding program. They can refer to it throughout the experience to keep each other on track. Build a document that spells out the roles and responsibilities of all the participants in the onboarding programs in your organization and then share it. In the sidebar below you'll find an example of an *Onboarding Process Partner Roles and Responsibilities Summary.* Although it may seem overly formal to lay out this type of document, it will serve as a touchstone as you start to develop who will do what actions throughout the process.

Human Resources Partner. An HR process partner is a member of the HR team who works most closely with the new employee to facilitate his or her onboarding process.

Role:

- Serves as the onboarding process guide for the new employee and functions as a guide and confidante.
- Facilitates the establishment of onboarding objectives, early wins, and the stakeholder analysis.
- Shares key documents and related insights with the new employee.
- Focuses on creating role clarity throughout the new employee's onboarding process.
- Facilitates the team alignment process (for new managers).
- Formally and informally gathers feedback regarding the new employee's effectiveness and assists in identifying and implementing solutions and developmental actions.

Hiring Manager. The manager of the new employee plays a critical role in the onboarding process.

Role:

- Serves as the primary information source regarding role expectations and direction of the new employee.
- Acts as the sounding board for the new employee and provides feedback and direction as the new employee learns about his or her role and the organization.
- Shares insight and advice about the employee's team and key stakeholders.
- Collaborates with the HR partner to ensure alignment of their actions throughout the new employee's onboarding process.

New Employee. The new employee is responsible for managing his or her onboarding process. While the hiring manager and HR partner will provide support and guidance, the new employee drives the overall process.

Role:

- Takes the initiative to work with his or her hiring manager to set and understand onboarding objectives, identify targeted onboarding meetings, and facilitate other transitioning activities.
- Reaches out to process partners when assistance is needed and is receptive to feedback and direction from those partners.
- Maintains a willingness to develop and demonstrate a deep understanding of and respect for the organization, its people, and practices.

There is a commercial running on television that shows a customer talking with his financial advisor. They finish the conversation, and the customer starts to walk away when a big, bright green line appears on the ground as he walks. Surprised, he turns around and asks his advisor about it, who tells him to "stay on the line" because that is his path to reaching the financial goals that the two of them just created. In one commercial, the customer walks out into the street, following his green line, but stops at a luxury car dealer to look in the window. The financial advisor looks out her door and down the street and motions the customer back to the green line. The customer looks a bit sheepish but happily returns to his path and walks on down the street. Think of the onboarding plan as the "green line" for new employees. It is the road map that keeps them and the organization focused on what's important and when it's important. There will be times when the employee or someone in the organization veers off the path and will need the help and feedback of someone to get him back on track, just like the financial advisor did for her customer.

Sample Onboarding Plan

Time Period	Actions	Resources
Prestart	Review the *New Hire Briefing Packet*	Links to company Web site
Week One	Logistical setup Attend orientation	New hire checklist
	Meet with manager	Agenda
	Understand company organization structure	Organization charts and year-end reports
Month One	Understand company financials Understand company language and acronyms Understand function's key processes	Monthly reports, project meetings
	Learn company strategy and key competitors	Sales and operations presentations

(continued on next page)

Time Period	Actions	Resources
Month One	Build relationships with key stakeholders	Personal network agenda
	Manage personal and family transition	Relocation specialist
Month Two	Assess the team	Performance reviews and interviews
	Participate in team alignment process	HR partner
	Learn how company measures performance	Balanced scorecard meeting
	Understand how each function operates within the company	Peer meetings
	Learn and embrace company's culture	Culture road map
Month Three	Participate in formal feedback process Continue to orient self and family to the area Develop/revise function's strategic plan	Survey
	Transition to performance management	Performance management on the intranet

Onboarding Plans Are Not Just Task Lists or Checklists

Let's take a look at what a typical onboarding plan might look like. Best practices suggest that the objectives are somewhat high level, time based, and have resources associated with them so that they can be carried out. It is important to note that an onboarding plan is not a task list or checklist. It identifies those key areas that the new employee should focus on, and there are usually several steps or tasks associated with the larger objectives.

So let's take an example of an objective and break it down into tasks, or "early wins" that will help the employee accomplish that objective. In month one, the first objective is "understand company financials." Because this is a broad objective, the employee will probably get started on it in month one but may not have the objective completed until later. There are several steps the employee will need to take to achieve this objective. First the employee must understand the company's financials and, for example, how the supply chain function can affect them.

Following are tasks or early wins that will help the employee accomplish this objective:

1. Review annual reports and company Web site.
2. Find a contact person(s) in finance who can provide the best overview as it relates to the supply chain.
3. Talk with team members to get their perspectives and hear about their experiences.
4. Attend meetings where financial results are reviewed.
5. Work on project team to launch product 2.0.

The new employee will also find that many of the tasks or early wins to meet certain objectives will overlap, and she can usually complete more than one objective at the same time. So, as she learns about the financials and how the supply chain affects them from a colleague in finance, she is also beginning to build a key cross-functional relationship with that someone or more than one person in finance.

As the new employee works on the onboarding plan, she starts to accomplish three main objectives in the process: gaining *knowledge* about the organization, the function, and her role; building key *relationships* that will help her achieve her objectives; and getting *feedback* that will allow her to know how she is fitting into the culture. These are the three most important components of a successful onboarding experience, and they set the stage for performance success as well. Too often, when these are lacking, the performance will slip, and issues will surface early. The feedback on a new employee will start to be, "She is not getting it," or "He is a bad fit," or "She was not the right hire for the job." Then unfortunately, the team and the organization will have to manage the situation by either working around that person or confronting the situation with a corrective plan, replacement, or both. This costs the organization both time and resources that could have been saved if the onboarding had been implemented successfully.

STEP TWO: MANAGE THE PLAN

It's great to have a plan, but the key to any successful plan is to execute it and to make changes and adjustments as you go along. The manager should be meeting with the new employee regularly, at least every other week, and weekly, if possible. This allows for frequent check-ins and alignment of priorities, questions, and clarification so that there is little chance of misunderstanding at this critical time. One of the most important relationships to develop for the new employee during his first 90 days is with his manager. It is also important that he develop good rapport with his coworkers and his customers, but if he is not aligned with his manager, then those other relationships will not be as important. He will also be able to learn about the culture from his manager and stay on track in achieving those onboarding objectives that are outlined in the plan.

The onboarding plan should also be used as the agenda for these check-in meetings. This will give the meetings both structure and consistency. It will allow the manager to track progress and decide when and if objectives have been met and if additional resources are needed to get them accomplished. It also can be used when it is time to wrap up the onboarding period and transition to the performance management process, as objectives can be transferred from the onboarding plan to the annual performance review.

STEP THREE: GIVE FEEDBACK EARLY AND OFTEN

As coaches and human resources consultants, we are often asked how particular situations could have been avoided or how good employees could have been "saved." And the answer we usually give is *feedback*. But it is not just the feedback itself, it is feedback done right and given at the right time to make a difference. It really is shocking to see how many managers avoid giving their employees the feedback they need when positive or negative behaviors or

Onboarding versus Performance Feedback

Onboarding feedback as part of a structured onboarding process is different from performance feedback. It allows the new employee to see specifically how he is or isn't integrating into the culture of the organization. Onboarding feedback is not only about the deliverables of the job and the metrics that are typically used in performance management, but it is also about how well the new employee is integrating into the new role, as well as how others are perceiving him. This doesn't mean, however, that the feedback is not data-oriented. Surveys that measure fit and gather data about perceptions and conversations with peers, team members, the new employee's manager, and any other key stakeholders can collect hard evidence of how a new employee is transitioning and integrating into the job.

performance issues occur. In the context of the onboarding experience, it is critical to set the stage for feedback early and often. It allows the new employee to get used to the idea that her new organization and culture do provide feedback, both in positive and constructive forms and is committed to doing so to make her more successful in her job. The old "no news is good news" just doesn't work anymore. This is especially true for the younger generations

Five Key Steps to Building Feedback into the Onboarding Experience

1. Match metrics to objectives.
2. Collect quantitative and qualitative data.
3. Include all participants.
4. Collect data as early as 45 days and no later than 60 days from the new employee's start date.
5. Report results both for how well the individual is onboarding and how effectively the organization is supporting the new employee's onboarding.

such as Gen X and Gen Y. They were raised on feedback and lots of it (mostly positive, so that can be a bit of a challenge), but they demand it, so managers must be ready.

The new hire who is not aware of his mistakes will continue to make them if no one is pointing them out. The result can be lost time, bad decisions, damaged relationships, and even failure. "Drive-by" feedback is also pretty common and is found mostly in hallway conversations or other informal settings. This may be a brief comment by the new employee's manager or peer without context or further explanation as to why a particular behavior or action didn't fit. The new employee is left with more questions than he had before he received the feedback and may be unsure as to what to correct or how.

Tips for Collecting and Giving Onboarding Feedback

- Put feedback topics on meeting agendas.
- Set aside enough time to have a good conversation.
- Do not save a sensitive topic for the end of a meeting.
- Be honest and direct but kind.
- Assume innocence and listen to why the behavior occurred.
- Solicit specific feedback from peers, customers, and other stakeholders to deliver to new employees.
- Describe the behavior and its impact on the organization, the team, or an individual.
- Send out short confidential e-mail surveys to key stakeholders such as team members, peers, and the manager.
- Ask questions of key stakeholders in private and in public to solicit good data.
- Practice active listening.
- Ask open-ended questions.
- Offer resources to support development.

Secondhand and humorous feedback are just as ineffective as drive-by feedback because they also lack context or examples to help the new employee understand why something he did may have been out of line. One example might take the form of, "I heard you really let them have it in that budget meeting!" Is that a good thing or a bad thing? The employee is left to decide for himself and doesn't always come to the right conclusion. The most common results of these typical kinds of feedback for new employees are confusion, frustration, disillusionment, misperceptions, and performance issues. All can contribute to an alarming failure rate of new employees.

SUMMARY

Onboarding can be the first important (and rather easy) step in setting up employees for long-term success. Establishing a standard of meeting objectives, building strong relationships, delivering results, and acting on feedback will provide employees with a solid base on which to develop their careers. If this is done well and embraced by both the employees and the organization, then performance will probably not be an issue, and development and succession planning will be more of the conversation in employees' annual reviews.

Chapter 2

The Four-Step Model to Getting Performance Management Right Every Time: Start Where You Are

We do not have the advantage of starting with a clean slate with our current employees. We need to start where we are and learn how to have productive conversations with employees to address performance. So this is our opportunity to "squash" the excuses listed in the Introduction that leaders often make, such as I don't have time, the employee should know this is a problem, and "I tried, and nothing changed."

Organizations that are best-in-class have several things in common: one of the most important common items is a structured, scalable process for having effective conversations that address performance challenges. Most organizations assume that their leaders know how to have these conversations and leave them to their own devices to get it done. Obviously, these organizations are "rolling the dice" at best and setting their leaders and employees up for failure at worst. This can be avoided by using a model that fits your organization and is intuitive for leaders.

Once leaders have a tool and receive training on how to use it, which makes their job easier and gets results, it will catch on like wildfire.

Before we outline our four-step model, let's define the roles and responsibilities of each of the three key players: leader, HR partner, and employee.

THE LEADER, THE HR PARTNER, AND THE EMPLOYEE

Of course the leader needs to take the lead, have the tough conversations, and hold the employee accountable for acceptable performance. However, the employee himself has a role and responsibility as does the human resources (HR) partner. Let's take a closer look at success factors for each role.

THE LEADER

As we said, the leader plays the lead role; she needs to be the driver and owner of managing performance issues. We are providing the leader with a four-step model and conversation preparation and discussion templates to use as tools for gathering the facts and ensuring that she is well-prepared for the conversation. An additional responsibility for the leader is to understand the policies and practices of her organization:

- What are the dos and don'ts of managing performance at your company?
- What is the progressive discipline policy, and when is it time to use it?
- What should be documented, and what do you do with your documentation?
- Did the employee violate a policy?

THE HR PARTNER

This is where the *human resources professional* role comes into play. The role of the HR partner is to provide guidance and support for the leader. In addition, the HR partner's role is to provide coaching and guidance around effectively preparing, delivering, and documenting performance conversations that are consistent with the organization's policies and practices.

By partnering with an HR partner, leaders protect themselves, become knowledgeable about the company's practices, and gain practice and confidence in having performance conversations.

THE EMPLOYEE

Let's not forget that *the employee* also has responsibilities and a role to play. The employee is responsible for meeting with his leader and engaging in the conversation. The most common mistake employees make is to get defensive. As we all know, when we feel defensive, we do not have an open mind, and we are not actively listening. Of course an experienced leader will notice if an employee is defensive and help to keep the conversation on track. Here are a few tips to help keep employees engaged in the performance conversation:

- Be purposeful about where you have the discussion and how and where you sit.
- Choose a private place.
- Do not sit across a desk from the employee.
- Manage your nonverbal communication.
- Acknowledge the employee's reaction.
- Focus on behaviors.
- Take a break if necessary, but only for a brief period.

It is very important to understand the roles and to keep them balanced. When the roles are not balanced, the performance conversation has a higher chance of becoming an employee relations problem.

Using the definitions and responsibilities outlined above for each of the three roles—leader, HR partner, and employee—the following illustrate examples of a balanced employee performance conversation and the consequences of unbalanced conversations.

Balanced Performance Conversation

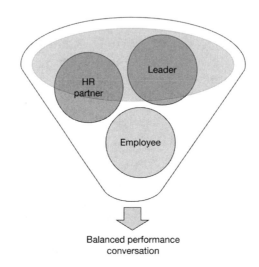

Balanced performance
conversation

Unbalanced Performance Conversation 1

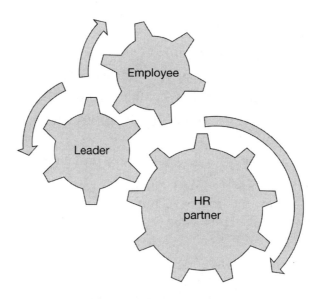

Consequences of the HR Partner Playing a Dominant Role

- Employee may not believe the leader has authority; employee does not feel he is accountable to the leader.
- Focus is on policy or practice rather than on behavior and performance.
- When the HR partner plays a dominant role, the leader does not have the opportunity to gain experience and confidence leading performance conversations.

Unbalanced Performance Conversation 2

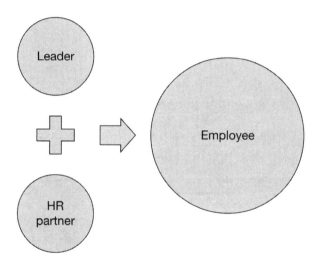

Consequences of the Employee Playing a Dominant Role

- Leader loses control of the performance conversation and employee.
- Focus is on the employee's perspective, which may not be accurate.
- Outcomes are unclear.

Unbalanced Performance Conversation 3

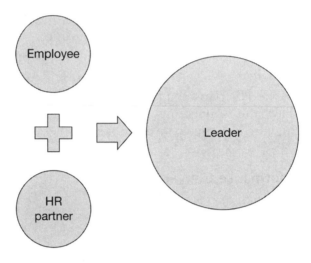

Consequences of the Leader Playing a Dominant Role

- Leader may be out of step with company policies and practices.
- Employee's view is not considered.
- Leader may not be effective in delivering the intended message.

A balanced approach to employee performance conversations positions the leader and employee for success. If one role is more dominant than another, the conversation has a higher chance of not meeting objectives and leading to an employee relations or more serious performance issue.

Knowing *what* to do is critical; knowing *how* to do it is just as important.

Now that the roles and responsibilities are clear, our next step is to explain our four-step model that gives each role a structure for successfully managing performance challenges.

Our proven, straightforward model and accompanying template for managing common and tough performance issues are tools that leaders find relevant and get the results they need—as long as they have the skills to effectively deliver the conversation. We cover this next.

WHAT TO DO: THE FOUR-STEP PERFORMANCE MANAGEMENT MODEL

The model below illustrates the four recommended steps of performance management.

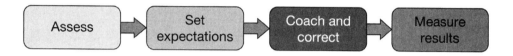

Let's walk through each of the components of the model.

1. STEP ONE: ASSESS

The first step in the model is to assess the situation.

Definition

It is important for the leader to assess the situation before making a decision or judgment that may not be correct. In order to assess the situation you must gather information that gives you a clear understanding of the "current state" of the employee's performance. Examples include:

- Work samples
- Project and task results
- Input from coworkers and customers
- Your experience with the employee
- Validated perceptions and/or secondhand information

Importance

Leaders sometimes act on hearsay or make assumptions that are not accurate. Leaders may also jump to conclusions and make decisions based on incomplete information. This of course has several consequences:

- Angry employee
- Eroded relationship and trust
- Potential employee relations issues

Once the assessment step is complete, a leader may discover that the issue does not exist.

Leaders need to have as much information as possible to effectively understand, communicate, and address performance issues. Otherwise the conversation can easily turn into an argument, or the employee disengages. Neither situation is desirable.

Example

Performance issue: Missing project deadlines.

Assessment

- Outline projects the employee was responsible for in the previous three months.
- Which projects were complete by the deadline, and which were not?
- Were there extenuating circumstances when deadlines were missed?
- Did the employee communicate that the deadline would be missed?
- Was the work done correctly?
- What are the employee's work habits?
- How is the employee's overall performance?

Clearly summarize how things are with the employee based on your objective assessment.

Dos and Don'ts for Assessment	
Do	**Don't**
Be timely	Wait until the issue is either old news or too far gone to resolve
Be objective	Act on perceptions, partial information, or hearsay
Consider the employee's perspective	Make assumptions

2. SET EXPECTATIONS

The second step in the model is to clearly set expectations.

Definition

To set expectations is to establish the work outcomes for which the employee is responsible. We all know the adage "you make an _ss out of you and me when you assume." Most leaders assume they clearly communicate the performance expectations on which they will measure an employee's performance. However, employees are often confused or have an incorrect understanding of what they need to achieve.

A 2008 article from the Society of Human Resources Management indicates that 40 percent of employees say that their leaders do not set clear expectations and that they do not know what their leaders expect from them.

A high percentage of performance problems could be avoided if leaders would take the time to clearly set expectations. As we discuss in Chapter 1, this starts with onboarding when the employee is new in his position, and it continues throughout the employee's tenure with the company.

It is obviously unrealistic and unfair to expect a team member to deliver results he is unaware of—no matter how obvious they may seem.

Using the familiar tried-and-true SMART (specific, measurable, attainable, result-focused, and time-bound) acronym gives you a tool to clearly set expectations as well as to provide the foundation for measuring success.

How do you know whether or not expectations have been met if the expectations haven't been clearly defined? Test the expectation against the SMART acronym:

- Is it specific?
- Can you measure whether or not the expectation was met?
- Is the expectation attainable for the employee?

- Is the expectation result-focused?
- Has a time frame been established for the performance expectation(s)?

Using the attributes of the SMART acronym takes away the ambiguity and assumptions.

Importance

Setting clear expectations gives both the leader and the employee the opportunity to deliver results and avoid wasting time and damaging relationships.

Example

"It is important that monthly reports are completed and submitted to me by the fifteenth of each month by the end of the business day."

| Dos and Don'ts for Setting Expectations ||
Do	Don't
Clearly communication your expectations	Assume that the expectations are obvious
Use the SMART acronym	Use vague terms such as always, never, sometimes, or improve
Confirm understanding	Assume you were clear

3. COACH AND CORRECT

The leader's job is not complete once the expectations have been clearly communicated. The leader needs to provide feedback on progress, training, support for dealing with barriers, and corrective feedback along the way.

Our model is cumulative. By assessing the situation to determine the current state and then clearly setting expectations, the leader can coach and correct based on the objectives.

Definition

To coach and correct the leader must provide the employee with feedback and direction regarding her performance on a specific assignment (expectation). Coaching and correcting need to reinforce positive performance and correct behaviors and/or performance that is not aligned with the agreed-upon expectations.

Importance

Coaching and correcting is a critical step that gives the leader and employee the opportunity to further develop their relationship, better understand how the other works, build the employee's confidence, and allow the leader to understand and address issues.

Example

"Let's review your work on the most recent reports. Walk me through the process you used, and I'll provide some feedback and suggestions."

Dos and Don'ts for Coaching and Correcting	
Do	**Don't**
Schedule coaching updates	Leave the employee on his or her own
Use coaching conversations as an opportunity to motivate	Assume that no news is good news

4. MEASURE RESULTS

If the leader has actively managed the first three steps, the fourth is "a piece of cake."

You should have a clear understanding of how the employee is doing, whether or not she or he is on track to deliver results, and why or why not.

Definition

Measuring results means that the leader must determine the results that have been achieved within a specific time frame. The leader must decide whether or not the expectation for performance has been met.

Importance

If the expectations were not clearly established, it will be much more challenging to measure what has been accomplished.

Example

"You have done a great job submitting the results no later than the fifteenth of each month in the past four months. This allows the other department to access the information they need to create operational reports."

Dos and Don'ts for Measuring Results	
Do	**Don't**
Use this step as an opportunity to motivate the employee and reinforce positive performance	Focus only on the negative
Stay focused on the agreed-upon expectations and deliverables	Add deliverables or expectations at the last minute

HOW TO DO IT

We now cover the *how*, as in how to effectively have the performance conversation using the template. The only way to become skilled at these conversations is the same as any other new skill such as skiing, playing golf, or closing the books—practice, practice, practice!

Many of you will be familiar with the learning model below:

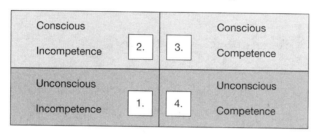

Most leaders truly begin in the first quadrant but think they are in the third quadrant. The only way to move from the first to the third or fourth is by practicing and getting feedback.

Most of us learn best by working through an actual situation that we need to address or manage. Take a moment to identify a performance conversation that you need to have. Use the template below to outline the situation. We will return to it shortly.

Conversation Prep Template

Performance situation
Consequences of the performance situation
Consequences of not addressing the situation
Timing for the conversation
Notes

It is critical to practice creating the content of the conversation using the template *and* how to deliver that content. You can have all the right words on the page; however, if you do not deliver those words in a way that communicates your intended message, the conversation misses the mark and potentially does more damage than good. Many leaders make the mistake of spending a "ton of time" on the words and little to zero time on delivery—big mistake.

Keys for Successful Delivery

- Be prepared:
  - How can you best communicate with this person?
  - Anticipate reactions and responses.
- Manage your nonverbal communication.
- Manage your "hot buttons."
- Focus on the issue—don't make it personal.

So how do you practice both content and delivery? Start with the small stuff. We all have opportunities to give feedback and address performance almost daily. So what are those situations that perhaps are let go today that should be dealt with, thus preventing a bigger issue down the road and creating a culture that is comfortable with feedback?

Following are some examples of small stuff that employees do that you can address to help you practice your delivery:

- Coming in a "few" minutes late two to three days a week
- Regularly extending breaks by a "couple" of minutes
- "Disappearing" from the work area for extended periods a few days a week
- Appearing "uninterested" at the last three staff meetings
- Arguing with coworkers over trivial issues

Because today's leaders have a wide range of responsibilities, less staff, and more complex "scorecards," many tend to ignore what seem like small, insignificant performance issues that may turn into larger issues. These issues are also opportunities to practice having performance conversations.

Go back to the conversation prep template. Is the situation you described addressing a small or big issue? If you are uncomfortable with performance conversations and need more practice, start with a few small issues, get comfortable, and find your voice.

The template gives you:

- Structure
- Asks you to plan
- Sets you up for a successful conversation

Once the conversation takes place, it is important to review how things went, were the objectives met, did the employee get the intended message, and is she committed to improving? On the following page, you'll see we've added review components to our template. By reviewing how the conversation went, leaders have the ability to learn from mistakes, reinforce what went well, and build confidence for future conversations.

Discussion Template

Prepare for Discussion
Performance situation
Consequences of the performance situation
Consequences of not addressing the situation
Timing for the conversation
Notes
Postdiscussion Review
Did the employee "hear" the message?
What went well?
What did not go well?
Next steps

SUCCESS IS CONTAGIOUS

Leaders who are confident and consistently have performance conversations with team members build a "leadership brand" and culture of dealing with issues quickly and correctly. Team members will know and come to expect this type of action and these types of conversations—creating a culture of openness, feedback, and performance expectations.

SUMMARY

The objective of this chapter is to remind leaders to start at the beginning rather than jumping to conclusions or making assumptions that may get in the way of effective management performance. The *four-step model* and *discussion template* give leaders tools that, if used, require them to step back, assess the situation, set expectations, coach and correct, and measure results. Once leaders practice delivering thoughtful performance conversations, they not only effectively manage the performance of their own team members, but they also teach those team members how to do the same—creating a performance culture.

The next chapter gives leaders the tools they need to confidently communicate the performance challenge and manage a solution.

Chapter 3

Communicate Clearly and Often

Communicate, communicate, communicate! Many leaders make the mistake (without really thinking about it) of thinking that employees have a clear understanding of what they are being held accountable for and how they are being held accountable. The annual performance review process often includes the exercise of identifying organization and department goals and then individual goals. These goals are often never spoken of again—until the next performance review process. If the leader does not actively update and communicate performance expectations, he is potentially leaving a large gap between his understanding of the performance each of his team members will be held accountable for and that team member's understanding. So how can leaders and employees bridge that gap and get in sync?

BITE-SIZED CHUNKS OF WISDOM FROM THE BEST

The ideas and practices in this chapter come from world-class organizations and their leaders—all noticeably effective in their leadership styles. All have proven track records when it comes to creating high-performing workplaces and conducting business in a way that actually helps prevent employee performance problems from growing, thereby, creating a platform for peak performers to launch ahead and sometimes even celebrate, or accept and discuss openly, their mistakes.

When it comes to developing the strategies that really breathe life into the workplace, there are lots of organizations that are doing it right. Throughout this chapter you'll find a bit about their philosophies and one-of-a-kind approaches to making it happen—bite-sized chunks of wisdom from the best in the business.

GETTING IN ALIGNMENT—THE POWER AND EFFECTIVENESS OF SYNCHRONIZATION

Leaders are responsible for continually trying to mind the gaps between the performance problems they may be experiencing and the high performance they are seeking. One way to accomplish this is for leaders to get their departments and their people in alignment.

This is more easily accomplished when everyone is in sync. Synchronization takes place when individual departments within an organization and employee expectations within those departments support the overall mission, vision, and goals of its leadership. In other words, everyone must be moving in the same direction and for the same reason, in order to get the same results.

The Ritz-Carlton Hotels (now a wholly owned subsidiary of Marriott International) are a perfect example of synchronicity and alignment in action. Ritz-Carlton considers this to be so important that synchronicity is practiced on a daily basis throughout the world.

Bite-Sized Chunks of Wisdom: The Ritz-Carlton Hotels

During a stay in Kansas City, Missouri, at The Ritz-Carlton, coauthor Anne Bruce interviewed then general manager Myra deGersdorff who explained how her award-winning organization takes strategy and performance to a higher level and how its 20 gold standards of performance and customer service pave the way:

During every shift, in every department, at 70 Ritz-Carlton properties around the world, more than 30,000 employees start their day by discussing the importance of one of the 20 Gold Standards, which by the way all employees carry with them on the job as a small folded card, practiced by the company. On that exact same day, every employee at The Ritz-Carlton Hotels around the world is discussing the same Gold Standard. When employees reach the twentieth Gold Standard, they start over again.

A few of the gold standard phrases include:

- To create pride and joy in the workplace, all employees have the right to be involved in the planning of the work that affects them.

- Each employee is empowered. For example, when a guest has a problem or needs something special, employees should break away from their regular duties to address and resolve the issue.

- Employees should take pride in and care of their personal appearance. Everyone is responsible for conveying a professional image by adhering to The Ritz-Carlton clothing and grooming standards.

Can you imagine the synchronicity an organization gains when all of its people are following and believing in the same goals and objectives at the same time, whether that be in London or in San Francisco? The Ritz-Carlton's efforts have paid off more than once, as winner of the prestigious Malcolm Baldrige National Quality Award—the first and only hotel company ever to receive such an honor.

GAUGING ALIGNMENT IN YOUR ORGANIZATION

What are you doing to mind the gap in your organization when it comes to improving performance? You can best gauge the alignment of people and their departments by taking the following actions:

- Ask employees to describe what performance, or success, looks like in their unit or department, based on the specific goals and objectives set by leadership. Departmental priorities and expectations of people should always add up to and support the organization's overall goals.

- Decide whether there are discrepancies between departmental and individual priorities. If so, work to close the gap for more unity and better focus. Use staff or other team meetings to discuss your findings and create an action plan. This establishes a dialogue about performance expectations and will keep your objectives relevant and clear to everyone.

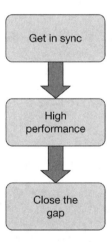

By asking employees questions about how they best achieve performance and success, leaders get their people to think through this process regarding the intricacies of the job. Questions to consider asking and that help excavate what an employee is thinking and feeling about his or her work, might include:

- What is challenging and most enjoyable about your work? How does this job make you stretch your talents to your higher level of potential and ability?

- What gives you job satisfaction and a greater feeling of purpose?

- To whom do you turn in a crunch? Where do you get your support?

- What are some of the obstacles you face when it comes to getting your work done? How have you handled those obstacles so far? What resources can you use that you don't presently have available to you?

- Are you getting the recognition you deserve?

- What motivates you intrinsically to your highest level of performance and productivity? Is it the feeling of a job well done? Being appreciated and rewarded for what you do? Being surrounded by leadership that walks the talk? Teamwork and collaboration with colleagues?

- What fuels you? How can I help facilitate your ongoing success?

By asking these questions and others, you will almost instantly be aligning people and departments with your organization's overall direction and performance standards. And as a bonus, you'll be creating strategic partners at all levels of the organization for ongoing higher performance and greater productivity.

Bite-Sized Chunks of Wisdom: Gallup

According to this highly reputable polling company, the greatest source of satisfaction and production on the job is rooted in both emotional and personal needs. Gallup's well-known Q12 research take on employee performance isn't about money or benefits, but rather *the quality of the relationship between employees and their supervisors.*

THE PERFORMANCE DIALOGUE

Just because you've verbalized something doesn't mean that you've communicated it. Merriam-Webster's Online (merriam-webster .com) defines communication as:

1. An act or instance of transmitting

2. Information transmitted or conveyed or a verbal or written message

3. A process by which information is exchanged between individuals through a common system of symbols, signs, or behavior
4. Exchange of information

Here is a basic communication model:

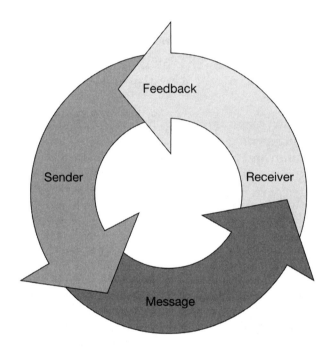

The model seems simple. Then why is communication often so complicated? What gets in the way? Assumptions.

Beware of Assumptions—They'll Throw You Off Track Every Time

Assumptions get us in trouble every time. Leaders are often surprised to find that their employees deliver work that is different from what they expected, or do *not* deliver work that they did expect. Even something as simple as, "Please get that to me as soon as possible," can be filled with misunderstanding. The leader is thinking in the next hour, and the employee is thinking after he completes two projects he is working on.

Leaders can avoid this common problem by communicating clearly and often, as well as by practicing active listening. As each new project or task comes up, think about the communication definition and model and answer each of the following:

- What is the purpose of the task?
- Who is the right employee for the task?
- What is the deliverable/performance outcome needed?
- What is the deadline?

Once you have answers to these questions, you are ready to communicate. Here's an example:

> *"Sophia, the sales group has asked us to pull together a report calculating national account discounts. The report needs to be sent to the sales manager by tomorrow at 3 p.m. I would like you to create the report. Let's agree to a plan to meet the deadline."*

Now that you have clearly communicated the performance expectation, it's your turn to actively listen to make sure that you and the employee are on the same page.

Keys to active listening are:

- *Summarize:* Ask the employee to summarize the assignment to make sure that he heard what you intended to communicate.
- *Do not interrupt:* Let the employee finish his sentences and ask questions.
- *Manage your nonverbals:* Maintain eye contact. Be purposeful about your facial expression and tone.
- *Summarize again:* Make sure you are both clear on the action plan.

You Think You Said It, but You Didn't

Today's leaders have broad responsibilities and are expected to deliver results quickly and accurately. This dynamic often makes it challenging to clearly communicate to all team members on a regular basis. As leaders move quickly through their days handling multiple projects, interruptions, and demands, they may make assumptions that they are communicating new information, changes in expectations, and different deadlines. They may think or assume that they passed on the information needed, but they may forget or assume that the employees got the information themselves.

To prevent these gaps in communication from happening, it is critical for leaders to make communication a core strength and focus. Leaders who are strong and consistent communicators and practice active listening build an environment in which team members have a clear understanding of the performance expectations for which they are being held accountable. These leaders work hard *not* to make assumptions, and they invest time and energy up front in order to prevent performance issues.

Bite-Sized Chunks of Wisdom: Nordstrom

The two most notable phrases from the highly popular retailer Nordstrom contain the following two rules:

1. Use your good judgment in all situations.
2. There will be no other rules.

REROUTE AND REDIRECT TO GET WHERE YOU WANT TO GO

How do leaders know if their team members understand their tasks and performance expectations?

Practicing active listening allows leaders to know if the employees have a clear understanding of the task or if they need to provide more information, address questions, or redirect the employees' focus. Leaders who do not actively listen have a much greater chance of making assumptions, missing information, and not getting the expected results.

Adding time-based check-ins is another way to ensure that the employee is on the right track to accurately complete the task. This of course is applicable for more complex tasks and projects.

Both of these techniques give the leaders and employees a high chance of meeting expectations and avoiding performance problems resulting from miscommunication.

Proactive communication is the key to effectively managing performance. The strategies and tools outlined in this chapter are designed to give leaders straightforward resources that can be integrated into their day-to-day work. Communication is often taken for granted and is often deemed the reason for our problems. Strong leaders are committed to developing their communication skills and proactively managing performance.

Bite-Sized Chunks of Wisdom: Amazon.com

Jeff Bezos continues to change the economics of the book industry with his vision for becoming a cyber bookstore with the world's largest selection. But all of this takes top performance and avoiding performance pitfalls. Here are a few Amazonian tips:

- Have clarity about your purpose. Top management must be able to answer the question, "Why are we here?"

- Know where you are going. Long-term strategies should come from the top.

- Ask where you are now. What are your strengths, weaknesses, opportunities, and challenges?

- Practice using a strategic planning triage. Identify short-term goals for the business that are consistent with the purpose and vision of the company.

- Develop strategies for each outcome. Strategies are broader efforts for achieving each of the core outcomes.

- Develop tactics. Tactics are step-by-step actions to be taken to achieve each strategy.

BE PROACTIVE: PREVENT EMPLOYEE PERFORMANCE PROBLEMS BEFORE THEY START AND COMMUNICATE CLEARLY AND OFTEN

Communications problems are cited in the top five reasons that couples divorce. And, not surprisingly, communications issues make

Bite-Sized Chunks of Wisdom: Virgin Group

Known for its wildly famous Gonzo Branding and the fabulous performance of its people, the Virgin Group comprises over 300 branded companies worldwide, employing approximately 50,000 people in 30 countries, and remains a most unusual combination of success and peak production. Most of its revenues come from financial services, media, airlines, megastores, mobile technology, fitness, and so on; the rest comes from hundreds of small ventures, like Virgin Cosmetics, Virgin Wines, and much more.

On March 30, 2000, Richard Branson, entrepreneur and founder of the Virgin Group became Sir Richard Branson. He was knighted for his services to entrepreneurship in a ceremony at Buckingham Palace. Branson is known for several compelling quotes and musings when it comes to achieving peak performance in one of his companies:

- Don't lead sheep, herd cats.
- Streamline decision making.
- Act as a catalyst.
- Encourage chaos.
- Make good ideas welcome (wherever they come from).
- Blur the divide between work and play.
- Never say never.
- Nice guys finish first.

the top five list for employee dissatisfaction and performance problems at work, according to Scott Carbonara, speaker, author, and former executive director of strategic communication and chief of staff of internal operations for a multi-billion-dollar health-care organization.[1]

Just as a marriage requires communication to survive and thrive, so does the workplace. Wise leaders understand that they must foster

[1] Visit Scott's Web site at www.ScottCarbonara.com and check out his popular book, *Firsthand Lessons, Secondhand Dogs*, a business book Scott wrote based on a dog he adopted and how the experience paralleled his experiences as chief of staff at a multi-million-dollar health-care organization and other life lessons.

trust, understanding, and engagement through a commitment to practice clear and frequent communication if they are to ward off potential employee performance problems.

If you suffer from a variety of employee performance problems in your workplace, you may want to take a look at the message you are communicating as a leader. At the heart of most employee performance problems is a communication gap. Did you know that when an employee suffers from performance problems, one of the most likely causes is a leader who has failed to communicate clearly, candidly, consistently, concisely, continually, and confidently? It's true. The most typical scenario might be that your employees *don't know what to do* or that they know what to do but *they don't know how to do it,* or *they lack the inspiration to do it.*

Scott Carbonara says that the best way to deal with employee performance problems is to prevent them from happening. In other words, be proactive, not reactive. Leaders who practice effective communication skills cut off problems before they have time to snowball into bigger ones.

AN EMPLOYEE PERFORMANCE PROBLEM COMMUNICATIONS TOOL KIT: USE THE *THREE I* APPROACH

Communication is the simple process of transferring information from one entity to another. Not exactly smashing atoms, right? Then why is it that communication can be enlightening, persuasive, and transformational at times, and a train wreck the next moment?

The difference lies in the effectiveness or clarity of the communication. According to Carbonara, clear and effective communication must employ the "three I" approach. That is, it must *inform, inspire,* and *influence.* See the following examples:

- *Inform.* "The office will be closing at 3 p.m. on July 3." Or, "This training session will give you the information you need to reach your goals."
- *Inspire.* "I want to give a special thanks to Jim who helped make this project so successful."

- *Influence.* "As this graph shows, our current system is unreliable and costly to repair. I think it's time to consider talking to vendors about a replacement." Or, "Wouldn't it be great if we could tap into this market? Who's with me?"

If communication succeeds in these areas, performance is enhanced. If it fails in any of these three areas, performance may falter. Consider these additional examples:

- A baby cries, *informing* its parents that it's time to eat. *Effective communication.*
- A dog sees a squirrel and barks, *inspiring* the squirrel to find another yard. *Effective communication.*
- A leader schedules a staff meeting, *influencing* all employees to attend; however, within minutes, the syncopated breathing of participants shows they have fallen into a deep slumber. *Ineffective communication!* The *inspire* part was neglected.

Bite-Sized Chunks of Wisdom: American Express

If you're going to try to prevent performance problems and create a workplace of cooperation, you need esprit de corps. American Express has many successful slogans from brand campaigns like "my life; my card" that have been parodied in hundreds of commercials by recognized names, such as Robert DeNiro, Tina Fey, Ellen DeGeneres, and Kate Winslet. Also touted for years was the company's well-known slogan of human performance and customer acceptance, "Membership has its privileges." It's no secret that when performance is the issue, group identity is key in this highly respected financial institution. The slogan also implies that when esprit de corps, or team spirit, is missing, productivity and success could suffer.

THE DIFFERENCE BETWEEN THE LIGHTNING BUG AND LIGHTNING

Mark Twain might have seen average communication compared with *truly* effective communication as the difference between the lightning bug and lightning. Ineffective communication shares similarities with noise pollution and television commercials: one-sided,

Bite-Sized Chunks of Wisdom: Whole Foods

Whole Foods is all teams when it comes to performance. It's also the largest natural foods grocery chain in the United States. Here are a few of its mantras and practices for removing misinformed conjecture and rumors that may hinder performance and productivity:

- All for one and one for all!
- Every team member at every level shall have access to the organization's operating and financial data.
- CEO's compensation is capped at 10 times the average team member's pay.
- Previous year's salaries and bonuses are posted by name for every employee.
- Only teams have the power to approve candidates for full-time employment, and it takes a two-thirds majority vote from the team to hire someone.

hard on the ears, and frequently ignored. In other words, it lacks inspiration or energy. The intent is there, but the effect is not. It flickers, but is not sustained.

Intending to communicate, but failing to achieve the desired effect, is not enough. Effective communication involves more than going through the motions of checking "I communicated" off a to-do list. Effective communication accomplishes specific, intended outcomes because its message and delivery compel others to listen, learn, and act. It provides needed information, as well as the lightning bolt that motivates employees to take action.

FOUR COMMON COMMUNICATION ROADBLOCKS

Carbonara points out four common communication errors of leaders:

1. *Leaders, themselves, may not know* how *to communicate.* Often, leaders are promoted for successes they had in previous roles, but they don't necessarily have leadership communication

skills. Michael Scott on television's *The Office* may have been the best salesperson in the history of Dunder Mifflin, but he lacked the communication skills to lead others effectively. Leaders may spend hours reviewing Key Performance Indicators and corporate scorecards, but if they can't translate what's in their heads to their employees, their employees are bound to have performance problems as they struggle to determine what is expected.

Solution: Learn how to communicate.

2.   *Leaders may not know exactly* what *to communicate.* In many large organizations, communication cascades down from senior leadership. Messages then get scrubbed by human resources, legal, and communication departments to the point that the resulting communication is devoid of any substance. In the end, leaders may not know the key messages; worse yet, they might miss the context of why it is vital that those messages be shared with their employees. Employees are left in the dark, often falling short of performance goals.

Solution: Be clear about the message before passing it along.

3.   *Leaders often retreat to Me-ville.* The population of the town of Me-ville experiences explosive growth when we focus on our own needs instead of the needs of those we lead. Being a leader doesn't bring immunity from fear and insecurity any more than being a parent brings knowledge of all of the answers. In times of change (e.g., economic downturns, layoffs, M&A activities), leaders often ask, "What's going to happen to *me?*" instead of, "What do my employees need from me?" Or, even better, "What can I do to support my organization during this time?" This causes employees to lose a level of engagement in their work.

Solution: Consider your employees' needs.

4.   *Leaders sometimes don't see communication as crucial to their job.* Productivity, quality, and costs are easily quantified. Most organizations create compensation structures and goals to improve these key metrics. Communication effectiveness, however, often falls off the radar for leaders. This proves to be shortsighted, because *what gets measured gets done.* If companies

spend millions of dollars gathering data for scorecards so that goals can be met and exceeded, why not create goals for communication and its effectiveness? Communication, while often an afterthought, does affect the bottom line: What is the cost of employee or customer turnover? How about the increased cost created by low engagement levels of employees? Or the exponential cost of dissatisfied, disloyal, and vocal employees or customers to your business? All these issues can be resolved by implementing proper communication.

Solution: Make communication a goal.

Bite-Sized Chunks of Wisdom: Intel

At Intel, values are at the heart of the company's production and people performance. In addition, Intel is an organization dedicated to improving the lives of its employees worldwide, both in and out of the office. When it comes to performance, Intel implements many of the following ideas and more:

- Assume responsibility.
- Execute flawlessly.
- Constructively confront and solve problems.
- Work as a team with respect and trust for each other.
- Be open and direct.
- Listen to all ideas and viewpoints.
- Do the right things right.
- Take pride in your work.
- Foster innovation and creative thinking.
- Embrace change and challenge the status quo.
- Ensure a safe, clean, and injury-free workplace.
- Make it easy to work with us.

Whether it's customer service, discipline, risk-taking, or executing ideas, Intel has lots of perfect phrases, including this one by Intel cofounder Robert Noyce, "Do not be encumbered by history. Go off and do something wonderful."

EIGHT STEPS TO PREVENTING EMPLOYEE PERFORMANCE PROBLEMS

From his years of experience in the communication field and his work as an author, researcher, and motivational speaker, Scott Carbonara developed a list of eight steps that great communicators practice. To be clear in your communication, follow these eight steps regularly.

1. USE STORIES TO INCREASE RETENTION AND AVOID FORGETFULNESS

Why is it that we can remember a joke that Jay Leno told last week or the details of Moses parting the Red Sea that we heard in Sunday school when we were 10 years old, but we struggle with recalling the content of a memo we just read—*twice*? Carbonara suggests that much business communication is fact and figure based. Jokes, parables, and anecdotes are stories.

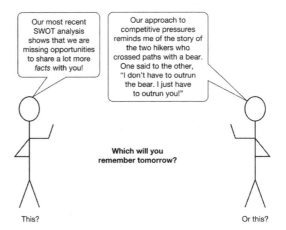

Facts get forgotten; stories get stuck. (S. Carbonara)

Perhaps your parents told you, "If you are known for lying, people won't believe you even if you are telling the truth." But wouldn't you be more likely to recall that lesson if it was packaged in story form, like in Aesop's fable, *The Boy Who Cried Wolf*? If you are trying to improve the ability of your audience to recall the moral of a story, you need a moral. And a story!

The Power of Storytelling

Imagine how early storytelling might have gotten its start. There's a group of cavemen sitting around a fire one evening. Many of the men participated in violent battles that took place earlier that day. First they battled a saber-toothed tiger and later a woolly rhinoceros. Suddenly one of the men leaps to his feet and begins communicating to the others what took place at the bloody scene. The caveman starts jumping up and down making sounds so graphic and compelling that no one speaks or moves. He's acting out the battle, waving his arms and gesticulating in a way that everyone sitting in the group begins to relive or "see" in their own minds what took place that day. The caveman is telling the story of what his group of hunters encountered that day, and everyone is captivated and terrified all over again.

One caveman then communicates to another that this cave dweller is no ordinary man and that there is magic in his words. So the cavemen take the storyteller away and kill him. Today that same riveting storyteller would be a successful company CEO or president—a famous twenty-first century leader, like Herb Kelleher of Southwest Airlines, Sir Richard Branson of Virgin Ltd, or Oprah Winfrey of the OWN Network. Their storytelling styles would be chronicled in top B-schools, like Kellogg, Stanford, Oxford, and Harvard, as required reading and case studies.

Carbonara used the power of storytelling when he was called in to deal with skyrocketing attrition problems within the customer service division of his organization. He interviewed several hundred employees who had voluntarily left the organization and documented their stories. At a meeting with the manager and officers of the division, Carbonara then told their stories.

"Let me tell you about Joan," he started. "She came to work for us six months ago because she believed in the vision of our company. But she quit last month. When I asked her why, she told me this: 'I would cry all the way to work and all the way home after work. It was a sweatshop with air-conditioning. My manager told me that if I didn't like it, I could leave at anytime because he could replace me tomorrow.'"

He told many more stories, all true, to communicate this one point to the leaders in the audience: "People aren't leaving our company. They are leaving *you,* their leaders."

Had Carbonara started the meeting by stating that attrition had reached 38 percent, would the leaders have found that fact useful? Had he told them that the annual cost of turnover in the service division had been conservatively estimated at 10 million dollars, would that have changed behavior? Had he begun with the conclusion that some leaders have forgotten how to care for and nurture employees, would they have listened?

No. But by telling a story, by pulling the leaders into the stress that their employees were feeling each day, attrition dropped to 6.5 percent within two years.

Employees who are told a story are more apt to take action to solve performance issues.

Bite-Sized Chunks of Wisdom: General Electric

GE is a company rich in history. Founded by Thomas Edison more than a century ago, former CEO Jack Welch inherited one of the world's most sacred institutions and applied some of the following perfect phrases to avoid performance problems while creating unprecedented, off-the-charts performance ratings during his reign:

- Don't be afraid to buck conventional wisdom.
- Avoid the minutiae.
- Don't think that you or your company has all the answers.
- Numbers aren't the vision. Numbers are the product.
- Never bully or intimidate.
- Don't punish yourself—or anyone else—for falling short of a stretch goal.

2. BE CONVERSATIONAL SO THAT EMPLOYEES WILL BECOME ENGAGED IN YOUR MESSAGE

During the 1996 presidential debates, Senator Dole and President Clinton presented different visions for the future of the country. Even more noticeable, they relied on two very different communication styles. Senator Dole was formal, stiff, and blunt in his answers. President Clinton was conversational, personable, and relaxed. Forget the politics: President Clinton's conversational style scored higher in each debate. And, of course, he won the election.

Much strategic communication reads like it was written in a boardroom by a gaggle of MBAs, because corporate messages usually are written by committees for the executive board or shareholders and not for "regular" people.

Most frontline employees don't have the "bandwidth" to embrace things like "leveraging synergies within the drill-down to find an integrated solution for added value to our end-users." But employees might get onboard if they were asked: "Can we come up with some ideas on our team to better serve our customers and other areas within the company?"

Employees who feel like they are part of a conversation instead of just a member of an audience tend to feel more vested in their performance.

Bite-Sized Chunks of Wisdom: Zappos

The famous e-tailer believes in the "psychic gratification" employees get from helping others. Call-center customer service reps are given tons of freedom—they are allowed to chat as long as they like with customers, write thank you notes, or even send flowers to a customer. Top priority? Make emotional connections so that people become engaged! CEO Tony Hsieh, who believes quirky is good, offers employees a list of his Ten Commandments, some of which include phrases such as:

■ Create fun and a little weirdness. (Parties in your PJs, parades, and shaved heads are part of the culture.)

■ Pursue growth and learning. (Employees are encouraged to study, read books, and take advanced training courses.)

3. USE REPETITION (WITHOUT BEING REPETITIOUS)

Writing and public speaking classes teach the same concept: tell people what you're going to tell them, tell them, and then tell them what you told them. Repetition helps people remember what you are communicating.

Depending on the message, it may be fine to use exactly the same phrase over and over to cement it in the minds of others. A superb example of this was used by the late Dr. Martin Luther King, Jr. His "I Have a Dream" speech is perhaps the greatest example of this technique.

It's also important that the message you repeat is succinct, direct, and positive. King didn't replace the "I have a dream" phrase with, "You know, I was thinking . . ." or, "Wouldn't it be great if . . . ?"

Carbonara used this method when developing the next level of customer service innovation in his organization, moving from transactional to customized, personalized customer service. Using both positive and negative examples as case studies in training classes for both frontline workers and their supervisors, he ended each example with this simple question: *Is this the way you would treat a loved one?*

Instead of investing time training on key points and behaviors of a complex plan to achieve customized, personalized customer service, Carbonara embedded a simple, repetitive question into the minds and hearts of the employees. This question became the mantra used any time a service representative saw a behavior that provided

Bite-Sized Chunks of Wisdom: eBay

eBay continues to build a worldwide culture of trust and high performance and uses these five basic principles of operation as its driving force:

- We believe that people are basically good.
- We believe that everyone has something to contribute.
- We believe that an honest, open environment can bring out the best in people.
- We recognize and respect everyone as a unique individual.
- We encourage you to treat others the way you want to be treated.

or did not provide the level of service an employee would offer a loved one.

Employees who hear consistent, clear messages are more able to act on them because they aren't distracted by the clutter of conflicting messages.

4. BE TRANSPARENT, HONEST, AND UP-FRONT

There's a link between how open you are as a communicator and how much your employees trust you. If you are closed or guarded, your employees might assume that you are hiding something. Nothing harms trust more than acting in a covert, secretive manner that leads others to believe you serve a hidden agenda.

With the exception of protected, private information, great communicators do not attempt to hold back; rather, they disclose as much information as they are empowered to share. This is especially important during times of change and insecurity, or when delivering bad news. Great communicators share information at the level necessary for others to act.

Employees who believe their leader are more likely to follow that leader.

Bite-Sized Chunks of Wisdom: Boston Consulting Group

This premiere, global management-consulting group, with more than 60 offices worldwide, practices transparent, honest, and up-front recruiting and onboarding practices. It has also greatly increased the recruitment of minorities, approximately 25 percent of the staff. Here are some of its credos:

- Believes no two career paths are the same.
- Offers formal training to support employees.
- Offers informal training to stretch employees.
- Initiates work-life balance with predictable time off.
- Takes a "grow further" approach to employee development.
- Believes that a person's potential is only limited by talents and ambitions.
- Provides experience to excel in numerous fields.

5. CONNECT THE DOTS

As a leader, your role is to point others to concepts, visions, and realities that are bigger than what they can comprehend today. The best leaders provide context, the *why,* surrounding certain events occurring within an organization. By connecting the dots for your employees, they better understand that their purpose is greater than what it might seem.

An oft-repeated story tells about a consultant working for NASA in the early days of the space program. As the legend goes, the man walked into the restroom and saw three janitors cleaning. He greeted the man closest to him with a nod and said, "How's it going?"

The janitor rolled his eyes in reply, "I clean toilets. How do you think it's going?"

The consultant blushed at the rebuke, and, out of nervousness, he automatically asked the same question to the next janitor: "Hi. How's it going?"

This janitor looked up with a little smile. "Oh, I can't complain. I'm feeding my family, you know," he said in a good-natured way.

As the consultant hurriedly left the restroom, he passed the final janitor who was smiling and humming while he scrubbed the floor. "Hi," the consultant said. "Why are you so happy?"

The third janitor replied with a grin: "Because I'm sending men to the moon!"

The third janitor performed janitorial duties just like the other two men working alongside him. However, his attitude and approach to his work was built on his belief of something bigger than the tasks he performed. His work performance shined because he carried a unique context for why his job mattered.

Carbonara points out that *context is decisive.* In the absence of credible, firsthand information to the contrary, people tend to draw their own conclusions about events based on their own personal experiences.

Many business messages *declare* facts: "We are moving our e-mail platform to Lotus Notes." "We are closing the Pasadena branch." "We are

Bite-Sized Chunks of Wisdom: IKEA

The hip and innovative Swedish furniture company banks on employee admiration and respect by keeping its global philosophies consistent and building pride within the organization—no matter what languages you speak. IKEA stakes its high performance and achievement on internal pride and enthusiasm using methods, such as:

- A code of ethics for its suppliers worldwide.

- Standing up for global child-labor protection laws.

- Seeking education for women and children in remote third-world countries.

increasing health-care premiums." The best communicators understand how to *declare* while providing *context* for why it all matters.

Employees who can connect the dots from their role to the big picture need less hand-holding to do their jobs well.

6. BE INTENTIONAL

Unless your goal is to test the limit of your spontaneity, you wouldn't drive to the airport and purchase a ticket for the first available flight to anywhere. Your goal (destination) dictates your plan.

Great communicators take the time to plan and launch communication that is purposeful. Armed with a clear purpose, great communicators craft messages that accomplish their desired goals. They anticipate how the audience will respond, and they mold the content to address the needs of the audience.

Once that message has been launched, great communicators make sure that it isn't forgotten like a sock behind the dryer. They take every opportunity to reinforce and update the message with memos, conversations, newsletters, blogs, tweets, electronic billboards, and so on.

Employees who have been given a clear, concise "call to action" act.

Bite-Sized Chunks of Wisdom: Pixar

The Academy Award–winning computer animation studio intentionally seeks super fun, tireless talent! Armed with clear and intentional purpose, Pixar knows the creative message it wants to craft that will engage people worldwide. Its priority? To combine technology with world-class creative talent and top-notch communicators. The creator of animated movies, such as *Finding Nemo*, *Toy Story*, and *Cars*, advertises on its Web site (using a creative spin on the *Cars* movie) that it is always looking to expand its pit crew of talented employees and that its "creative mechanics" come in all shapes and sizes.

7. LISTEN WITH INTENSITY

Carbonara believes that anyone can improve oral communication by practicing some simple, techniques:

- Make eye contact. (Don't stare at the other person's shoes.)
- Speak clearly and audibly. (Don't mumble or whisper.)
- Maintain a good pace. (Don't race to the finish or talk so slowly that the other person falls asleep.)
- Use words the listener understands. (Don't talk over or under the head of the listener.) However, great conversationalists comprehend the psychological elements of communication too.

As a former family therapist, Carbonara points out that psychologists are often considered great conversationalists and communicators. The very nature of the therapeutic, counseling relationship mandates that the therapist keep the discussion "all about you," all about the client. In *Firsthand Lessons, Secondhand Dogs,* where Carbonara shares life lessons taught by a dog he rescued from being euthanized, he surmises that the best leaders and greatest communicators understand how to attune their ears to *truly* listen to others.

Beyond the technical aspects of effective communication, Carbonara believes that the best communicators create psychological connections with others by using *high-intensity listening* more than any exemplary technical, writing, or speaking skills. One of the surest ways to improve the clarity and accuracy of your communication is to become known as a world-class listener.

Bite-Sized Chunks of Wisdom: Target

A performance-driven risk taker who works at Target, one of the nation's top retailers with more than 280,000 employees and locations in almost every state, will often use the following Target phrases to describe himself or herself:

- Loves fun and challenging work.
- Appreciates feedback because it contributes to professional development and growth.
- Wants to be part of a socially responsible organization that gives more than $2 million a week to the communities it serves.
- Has a great sense of individuality.
- Recognizes the importance of diversity.

A few Target corporate culture statements include: Whatever the experience, you are Target Corporation; and, You are excited and you should be.

Carbonara suggests these tips:

- Stick to the topic. (Don't jump into a conversation only to twist it and make it all about you.)
- Stay interested in what's being said. (Don't be thinking about what you're going to say next.)
- Ask open-ended questions to keep the conversation moving. (Don't ask yes or no questions, but rather, "How did you . . . ?" or "What do you think about . . . ?" questions.)
- Listen more; talk less. (Don't believe that you are more interesting than the person you're talking with.)

Employees who feel heard and valued usually say *thank you* by performing at a higher level.

8. PREVENT ONGOING PERFORMANCE PROBLEMS

In his book *Don't Throw Underwear on the Table & Other Lessons Learned at Work*, Carbonara reminds us that *feedback is our friend,* and those who share feedback with us present us with a most precious gift.

Bite-Sized Chunks of Wisdom: Microsoft

You might think that such a high-tech organization might be low touch when it comes to coaching employees for greater performance. Not so. Here are some of the phrases used by Microsoft when it comes to facilitating the success of its people in an amazingly fast-moving and enormously competitive industry:

- Challenge people's weaknesses by giving them new responsibilities.
- Give employees opportunities that expose them to upper-level management.
- Walk a mile in someone else's shoes. Let employees spend a day in another department to see what goes on and observe performance.
- Lead by example.

Many new managers tell themselves that the absence of criticism from their customers, bosses, peers, or employees is a sign that all is well. *The absence of feedback, however, is not the same as the presence of praise.* Leaders actively seek feedback, both criticism for things requiring improvement and praise for what's going well. Likewise, great communicators are not interested in having flawless oral and written communications from a "performance" standpoint. Rather, superior communicators spend much time making certain that their intended message is clearly and accurately being received by others.

The best communicators use every tool at their disposal to find out what people are saying, feeling, thinking, and experiencing. Even when using static communication channels such as memos, newsletters, and blogs, they create opportunities for two-way communication to occur. They supplement more static channels with dynamic ones, taking advantage of town hall meetings, staff meetings, and one-on-one conversations to receive additional feedback. That feedback is critical because it will help shape the next message.

Employees who are actively engaged in the feedback process have a vested interest in the outcomes.

WHAT NOW?

You've made your point using memorable stories, a conversational tone, appropriate repetition, honesty, strong context, intentional messages, and intense listening. All feedback indicates that your message has reached the saturation point with your intended audience.

If a leader with solid communication skills is unable to help an employee improve his or her performance after using these strategies, it's time to provide challenging corrective feedback to the employee about the next possible step for continued noncompliance with the standards: a consequence (e.g., "up to and including termination").

In the meantime, keep these communication tools sharp. You will use them continually throughout your life and career, because you are always communicating. With practice, you will be remembered as a leader who helped solve employee performance problems with good communication.

Chapter 4

Accelerate Performance Success: From 0 to 60 in Real Situations

The foundation has been laid, roles and responsibilities have been defined, and the next step is to leverage the foundation and practice managing performance using the four-step model.

It is important for leaders to be clear and direct when talking with employees about performance challenges. Failure to do so often brings about additional challenges and erodes trust between the employee and leader. Many times leaders are uncomfortable when having performance conversations; they are not sure what to say or how to say it. Or the leader believes that the employee should understand the need to change and correct himself or herself without the leader's involvement. However, it is the leader's responsibility to address and manage the performance of team members.

This chapter is designed to help the leader build confidence by providing structure and suggested language to enable practice having performance conversations. The chapter applies the four-step model to 19 performance challenges, including challenges that could lead to termination. The worksheets and templates provide suggested language to help the leader successfully address the performance problem with an employee and enable the leader to measure progress and hold the employee accountable.

PERFORMANCE MANAGEMENT WORKSHEET

The worksheet that precedes each performance challenge template is designed to:

- Define the performance challenge.
- List common reasons for the challenge.
- Give a sample SMART objective to address the challenge.
- Outline keys for the leader to follow in order to succeed in managing this performance challenge.

Use the following worksheets and templates to help you manage specific performance challenges.

BEHAVIOR AND CONDUCT PROBLEMS WORKSHEETS

Behavior and Conduct Problems Worksheet 1

Performance challenge	Inappropriate language
Definition	The employee uses language that is unprofessional and may be offensive to others. May include curse words, slang, or explicit terms or discriminatory language.
Common reasons for challenge	■ Professional inexperience ■ Person uses such language outside of work ■ Casual, informal work environment ■ Lapse of judgment
Sample SMART objective(s): ■ Specific ■ Measurable ■ Attainable ■ Results-focused ■ Time-based	Joe will immediately stop using inappropriate language in our workplace by self-managing the language that he uses. S: Stop using inappropriate language M: Inappropriate language is used or not A: Yes, Joe is able to attain this objective by self-management R: Inappropriate language is stopped T: Immediately
Keys for leader's success	■ Address the situation as soon as it happens ■ Be professional ■ Be direct and clear ■ Hold the employee accountable

Behavior and Conduct Problems Template 1

Performance challenge	Inappropriate language
1. Assess. Describe the following: ■ The performance challenge ■ The impact of the performance challenge ■ The required performance ■ Employee history	
Discussion opening: state purpose of discussion	Joe, the reason that I asked to meet with you today is to discuss a conversation I overheard (or feedback I have gotten) . . .
Describe your observations	When you were talking with Jill yesterday about the new policy we recently announced, you used language that's inappropriate in our workplace.
Describe your reactions	I was surprised to hear you use that type of language, and the look on Jill's face indicated that she was uncomfortable.
Give the other person an opportunity to respond	What do you think about this?
2. Set expectations: ■ Follow the elements of SMART to clearly outline performance expectations ■ Agree to an action plan	
Discussion	It's important that you understand that the language you used is inappropriate and will not be tolerated.
3. Coach and correct: ■ Give the employee direction and support needed	
Discussion	Joe, I can see that you're embarrassed, and I appreciate your commitment to never using inappropriate language in our workplace . . .
4. Measure results: ■ Based on the timeline established (set expectations), measure progress and results ■ Determine impact ■ Adjust expectations as appropriate	
Discussion	I don't expect to have this conversation with you again. However, if it comes up again, we'll need to take disciplinary action.

Behavior and Conduct Problems Worksheet 2

Performance challenge	Not meeting minimum job requirements
Definition	Employee is not performing her job at a satisfactory level.
Common reasons for challenge	■ Lack of understanding job requirements ■ Insufficient training ■ Not motivated
Sample SMART objective(s): ■ Specific ■ Measurable ■ Attainable ■ Results-focused ■ Time-based	Jill will begin to meet the minimum requirements of her job by the end of the week. Jill and I will meet each Friday to review her work and determine if she needs further training or if she has met the requirements. S: Will meet minimum job requirements M: Will track progress each week A: Training will be provided if Jill needs additional support R: Results will be measured T: By the end of the month
Keys for leader's success	■ Be specific; avoid vague language such as "sometimes" or "always" ■ Understand how to motivate the employee ■ Make sure your nonverbal communication "matches" your verbal messages

70

Behavior and Conduct Problems Template 2

Performance challenge	Not meeting minimum job requirements
1. Assess. Describe the following: ■ The performance challenge ■ The impact of the performance challenge ■ The required performance ■ Employee history	
Discussion opening: state purpose of discussion	Jill, the reason that I asked to meet with you today is to discuss your current performance.
Describe your observations	As we discussed last month, there are three core deliverables for which you are responsible and which we count on. In the last month your performance has not met our minimum requirements for accuracy and completeness.
Describe your reactions	After giving you individual training and coaching, I expected you to be able to meet the minimum requirements of your job.
Give the other person an opportunity to respond	What are your thoughts regarding your level of performance?
2. Set expectations: ■ Follow the elements of SMART to clearly outline performance expectations ■ Agree to an action plan	
Discussion	It's important that we establish a clear and measurable plan to address this performance challenge.
3. Coach and correct: ■ Give the employee direction and support needed	
Discussion	Jill, are you confident that you will be able to perform at the level I have outlined?
4. Measure results: ■ Based on the timeline established (set expectations), measure progress and results ■ Determine impact ■ Adjust expectations as appropriate	
Discussion	We'll meet every two weeks to review your progress in relation to the objectives we've set.

Behavior and Conduct Problems Worksheet 3

Performance challenge	Spreading gossip and rumors
Definition	Sharing false or speculative information or opinions about coworkers, management, or other stakeholders. This includes spreading rumors about possible policy, personnel, and company changes.
Common reasons for challenge	■ Lack of understanding or professional experience ■ Issues between coworkers ■ Lack of understanding or clarity ■ Lack of information during significant change
Sample SMART objective(s): ■ Specific ■ Measurable ■ Attainable ■ Results-focused ■ Time-based	Tim will immediately stop spreading rumors about a coworker. Instead Tim will meet with his coworker by the end of the week so that the coworker can explain his frustration. They will work together to address the problem. S: Stop spreading rumors and meet with the coworker M: Measure whether or not Tim stops spreading rumors and meets with his coworker A: Tim has the ability and support to achieve this objective R: Rumors will stop and the relationship between Tim and coworker is improved T: Immediately, by the end of the week
Keys for leader's success	■ Be specific ■ Be patient ■ Provide coaching ■ Hold employee accountable

Behavior and Conduct Problems Template 3

Performance challenge	Spreading gossip and rumors
1. Assess. Describe the following: ■ The performance challenge ■ The impact of the performance challenge ■ The required performance ■ Employee history	
Discussion opening: state purpose of discussion	Tim, the reason that I asked to meet with you today is to talk with you about an issue regarding you and one of your coworkers.
Describe your observations	As you know we work hard to create a sense of teamwork in our department. It has come to my attention that you may be involved in spreading gossip and rumors about a coworker.
Describe your reactions	Obviously this type of behavior is counterproductive to our goal of strong teamwork.
Give the other person an opportunity to respond	Please help me understand what is going on between you and your coworker.
2. Set expectations: ■ Follow the elements of SMART to clearly outline performance expectations ■ Agree to an action plan	
Discussion	It's important that we treat one another with respect and build a strong team. When you have an issue with a coworker, you're responsible for working it through productively.
3. Coach and correct: ■ Give the employee direction and support needed	
Discussion	Tim, you're a strong and important part of our team, I'm confident that you will handle conflicts with coworkers effectively in the future.
4. Measure results: ■ Based on the timeline established (set expectations), measure progress and results ■ Determine impact ■ Adjust expectations as appropriate	
Discussion	We will meet in two weeks to see how you are doing in dealing with your coworker. We'll make adjustments to our plan as needed.

Behavior and Conduct Problems Worksheet 4

Performance challenge	Politically incorrect behavior
Definition	Exhibiting behavior, including language, that may be offensive and/or make coworkers or other stakeholders uncomfortable.
Common reasons for challenge	■ Professional immaturity ■ Personal opinions or feelings ■ Unawareness of the feelings of others
Sample SMART objective(s): ■ Specific ■ Measurable ■ Attainable ■ Results-focused ■ Time-based	Immediately stop using slang or derogatory language about more mature, older employees in the workplace. S: Stop using . . . M: Measure whether or not the language or behavior stops A: The employee has the knowledge and ability to attain this objective R: The inappropriate behavior stops and improves the workplace environment T: Immediately
Keys for leader's success	■ Address right away ■ Follow up ■ Confirm understanding

Behavior and Conduct Problems Template 4

Performance challenge	Politically incorrect behavior
1. Assess. Describe the following: ■ The performance challenge ■ The impact of the performance challenge ■ The required performance ■ Employee history	
Discussion opening: state purpose of discussion	Mandy, I'd like to talk with you about your behavior toward your more mature team members.
Describe your observations	I've heard you make several inappropriate comments toward these team members, such as, "I bet they never had this kind of technology when you started working way back when!"
Describe your reactions	I'm disappointed that you're making these types of inappropriate comments, and I know that the comments make your team members uncomfortable.
Give the other person an opportunity to respond	Please help me understand why you make these types of comments.
2. Set expectations: ■ Follow the elements of SMART to clearly outline performance expectations ■ Agree to an action plan	
Discussion	It is critical that you stop making these inappropriate comments immediately. As we discussed, continued inappropriate comments will lead to progressive discipline. I appreciate your commitment to treating all of your team members with respect.
3. Coach and correct: ■ Give the employee direction and support needed	
Discussion	Mandy, I know that you want to be a positive team member, and I'm confident that you won't make any further inappropriate comments regarding your mature team members.
4. Measure results: ■ Based on the timeline established (set expectations), measure progress and results ■ Determine impact ■ Adjust expectations as appropriate	
Discussion	We'll meet again next Friday to talk about your progress on this critical behavior change.

Behavior and Conduct Problems Worksheet 5

Performance challenge	Under the influence at work
Definition	Employee is on the job after either drinking alcohol or using illegal drugs.
Common reasons for challenge	■ Poor judgment ■ Addiction
Sample SMART objective(s): ■ Specific ■ Measurable ■ Attainable ■ Results-focused ■ Time-based	Read our substance abuse policy and be ready to discuss it with me by 3 p.m. today. S: Read the policy M: Reading and understanding the policy A: The employee has the skills and direction to attain the objective R: Understanding of and compliance with the policy T: By 3 p.m. today
Keys for leader's success	■ Address immediately ■ Have a clear understanding of the policy ■ Partner with human resources

Behavior and Conduct Problems Template 5

Performance challenge	Under the influence at work
1. Assess. Describe the following: ■ The performance challenge ■ The impact of the performance challenge ■ The required performance ■ Employee history	
Discussion opening: state purpose of discussion	Paul, we need to talk about the condition you were in when you came to work on Saturday morning.
Describe your observations	Several of your coworkers have come to see me concerned that you were under the influence of either alcohol or illegal drugs during your shift.
Describe your reactions	Of course I'm very concerned and alarmed by what your coworkers described. It's both highly dangerous and against company policy to come to work under the influence. As you know, this could be grounds for termination.
Give the other person an opportunity to respond	What is your explanation for your behavior during your shift on Saturday?
2. Set expectations: ■ Follow the elements of SMART to clearly outline performance expectations ■ Agree to an action plan	
Discussion	As we've discussed, working under the influence is not acceptable under any circumstances. Our company policy is very clear, and you need to comply 100 percent with this policy. Failure to do so can lead to termination.
3. Coach and correct: ■ Give the employee direction and support needed	
Discussion	Paul, I know that this has been a difficult conversation. However, it's my responsibility to ensure that my team has a safe work environment. We cannot tolerate team members who are under the influence at work or who demonstrate behavior that causes team members concern.
4. Measure results: ■ Based on the timeline established (set expectations), measure progress and results ■ Determine impact ■ Adjust expectations as appropriate	
Discussion	We'll meet again next Friday to review our discussion, and I'll be stopping in on Saturdays to observe you.

WORK PERFORMANCE WORKSHEETS AND TEMPLATES

Work Performance Worksheet 1

Performance challenge	Lack of teamwork
Definition	Works independently; does not respond to or engage coworkers to exchange information and get work done.
Common reasons for challenge	■ Prefers to work independently ■ Does not feel comfortable with coworkers ■ Believes he can do it better on his own
Sample SMART objective(s): ■ Specific ■ Measurable ■ Attainable ■ Results-focused ■ Time-based	Create an action plan by Friday that outlines how you will work with your coworkers, John and Marcus, to complete next month's sales report. S: Create an action plan with your coworkers M: Measure whether or not the employee creates the action plan and carries it out A: The employee has the skills and direction to achieve the objective R: Improved teamwork between employee and coworkers T: By Friday
Keys for leader's success	■ Be clear and specific ■ Coach the employee to build understanding ■ Confirm understanding ■ Follow-up

Work Performance Template 1

Performance challenge	Lack of teamwork
1. Assess. Describe the following: ■ The performance challenge ■ The impact of the performance challenge ■ The required performance ■ Employee history	
Discussion opening: state purpose of discussion	Jake, I need to talk with you about your interactions with the other team members.
Describe your observations	I've noticed that you seem to prefer to work independently and use e-mail to communicate with other team members. This type of behavior demonstrates a lack of teamwork.
Describe your reactions	I'm concerned that a lack of teamwork between you and the rest of the team is having a negative impact on our productivity.
Give the other person an opportunity to respond	Please help me understand your perspective.
2. Set expectations: ■ Follow the elements of SMART to clearly outline performance expectations ■ Agree to an action plan	
Discussion	It's important that you demonstrate that you are a team player and can work effectively with other team members.
3. Coach and correct: ■ Give the employee direction and support needed	
Discussion	Jake, now that I have a better understanding of how you prefer to do your work and you are clear about the importance of teamwork, I believe you will make the necessary adjustments to become a strong team member.
4. Measure results: ■ Based on the timeline established (set expectations), measure progress and results ■ Determine impact ■ Adjust expectations as appropriate	
Discussion	We'll meet every two weeks to review your progress with respect to the objectives we have set.

Work Performance Worksheet 2

Performance challenge	Not demonstrating leadership
Definition	Does not set clear performance expectations or manage employee behavior.
Common reasons for challenge	■ Does not understand leadership behavior ■ Focuses on operational or technical aspects of job ■ Is unclear on how to carry out leadership responsibilities ■ Does not want to have leadership responsibilities ■ Needs training and coaching
Sample SMART objective(s): ■ Specific ■ Measurable ■ Attainable ■ Results-focused ■ Time-based	Outline your understanding of your role and responsibilities as a leader by next Wednesday. S: Outline understanding of role and responsibilities M: Assess whether or not employee has completed outline A: Employee has the ability to complete the outline R: Assess whether or not Sarah understands her leadership responsibilities and what the appropriate next steps are T: By next Wednesday
Keys for leader's success	■ Be clear about leadership performance expectations ■ Provide coaching and direction ■ Be patient

Work Performance Template 2

Performance challenge	Not demonstrating leadership
1. Assess. Describe the following: ■ The performance challenge ■ The impact of the performance challenge ■ The required performance ■ Employee history	
Discussion opening: state purpose of discussion	Sarah, the reason that I asked to meet with you today is to talk about a concern I have about your comfort with the leadership aspect of your role.
Describe your observations	I've noticed that on several occasions in the past two months you haven't outlined expectations or held team members accountable for deliverables.
Describe your reactions	This suggests to me that you may not be comfortable with your role as a leader.
Give the other person an opportunity to respond	How do you feel you are doing as a leader?
2. Set expectations: ■ Follow the elements of SMART to clearly outline performance expectations ■ Agree to an action plan	
Discussion	It's important that we establish a clear and measurable plan to address your leadership responsibilities.
3. Coach and correct: ■ Give the employee direction and support needed	
Discussion	Sarah, I know that you're capable of performing the leadership behaviors we have discussed. It's important that you begin executing the plan we've outlined.
4. Measure results: ■ Based on the timeline established (set expectations), measure progress and results ■ Determine impact ■ Adjust expectations as appropriate	
Discussion	We'll meet every two weeks to review your progress in relation to the objectives we have set.

Work Performance Worksheet 3

Performance challenge	Lack of follow-up and follow-through
Definition	Employee does not respond to requests for information, deliver information or perform tasks that she is committed to, nor does she get back to coworkers and other stakeholders regarding complaints and problems.
Common reasons for challenge	■ Heavy workload ■ Forgetfulness ■ Lack of organization ■ Lack of engagement
Sample SMART objective(s): ■ Specific ■ Measurable ■ Attainable ■ Results-focused ■ Time-based	Draft a suggested system that you can use to address your issue with follow-up. Be prepared to share your draft with me during our weekly meeting on the tenth. S: Create a draft of a solution M: Determine whether or not the employee completed the draft A: The employee has the knowledge and skills to create the draft R: Create a solution for addressing the performance challenge T: Complete the draft by the tenth
Keys for leader's success	■ Confirm understanding of the performance challenge ■ Coach to create a final solution ■ Hold the employee accountable for acceptable performance

Work Performance Template 3

Performance challenge	Lack of follow-up and follow-through
1. Assess. Describe the following: ■ The performance challenge ■ The impact of the performance challenge ■ The required performance ■ Employee history	
Discussion opening: state purpose of discussion	Mark, the reason that I asked to meet with you today is to talk about a problem you've had with follow-up in the past three weeks.
Describe your observations	I've given you four production irregularities to research in the past three weeks and have not received any information or questions from you regarding these assignments.
Describe your reactions	I'm surprised that you haven't followed through on these assignments. I'm also frustrated that we're now behind schedule on this work.
Give the other person an opportunity to respond	Can you please help me understand why you haven't followed through on any of these projects?
2. Set expectations: ■ Follow the elements of SMART to clearly outline performance expectations ■ Agree to an action plan	
Discussion	It's important that we establish a clear and measurable plan to address your lack of follow-up.
3. Coach and correct: ■ Give the employee direction and support needed	
Discussion	Mark, I'm confident that by following the plan we've outlined, you'll get back on track and have a plan for following up on research projects in the future.
4. Measure results: ■ Based on the timeline established (set expectations), measure progress and results ■ Determine impact ■ Adjust expectations as appropriate	
Discussion	We'll meet every week to review your progress in relation to the objectives we've set.

Work Performance Worksheet 4

Performance challenge	Substandard customer service
Definition	Employee is not delivering an acceptable level of customer service to either external or internal customers. May include behaviors such as not responding to customers in agreed-upon or acceptable time frames, not using appropriate language or tone, or not following through on issues.
Common reasons for challenge	■ Burned-out ■ Lack of training ■ Not fit for a customer service role ■ Unclear expectations
Sample SMART objective(s): ■ Specific ■ Measurable ■ Attainable ■ Results-focused ■ Time-based	Beginning immediately, use our five-step process when dealing with customers. I will randomly listen or observe your customer interactions to ensure that you are delivering acceptable customer service. S: Use our five-step customer service process M: Measure level of success through observation of customer interactions A: Employee has the tools and training to achieve required performance R: Results in acceptable customer service T: Beginning immediately
Keys for leader's success	■ Provide training on customer service expectations ■ Observe employee and provide feedback ■ Motivate employee based on his style ■ Hold employee accountable

Work Performance Template 4

Performance challenge	Substandard customer service
1. Assess. Describe the following: ■ The performance challenge ■ The impact of the performance challenge ■ The required performance ■ Employee history	
Discussion opening: state purpose of discussion	Megan, I need to talk with you about the level of customer service you have been providing to your customers in the past 30 days.
Describe your observations	Three of your customers have contacted me to complain about the level of service you've been providing. In addition I've listened to five of your customer calls. You were short, and your tone of voice indicated you did not want to be on the call.
Describe your reactions	I'm disappointed by your recent lack of customer service. It is critical that you make significant improvement immediately.
Give the other person an opportunity to respond	Why has your customer service level dropped in the past 30 days?
2. Set expectations: ■ Follow the elements of SMART to clearly outline performance expectations ■ Agree to an action plan	
Discussion	It's important that we establish a clear and measurable plan to address your level of customer service skills.
3. Coach and correct: ■ Give the employee direction and support needed	
Discussion	Megan, I understand that you have a challenging job. I also know that you are capable of delivering consistently high levels of service to your customers.
4. Measure results: ■ Based on the timeline established (set expectations), measure progress and results ■ Determine impact ■ Adjust expectations as appropriate	
Discussion	We'll meet every week to review your progress in relation to the objectives we've set and customer feedback.

Work Performance Worksheet 5

Performance challenge	Unacceptable error rate
Definition	Employee's work consistently has a high number (needs to be defined) of errors.
Common reasons for challenge	■ Lack of knowledge or training ■ Lack of attention to detail ■ Works too quickly
Sample SMART objective(s): ■ Specific ■ Measurable ■ Attainable ■ Results-focused ■ Time-based	It's critical that each month-end sales report does not have any financial errors. S: Zero errors, each month-end sales reports M: Count the number of errors in each report A: Employee has the knowledge and skills needed to accurately prepare month-end reports R: Error-free month-end reports T: Monthly
Keys for leader's success	■ Ask open-ended questions to gain an understanding of why employee is making errors ■ Explain how errors affect other departments ■ Provide appropriate training ■ Give feedback each month

Work Performance Template 5

Performance challenge	Unacceptable error rate
1. Assess. Describe the following: ■ The performance challenge ■ The impact of the performance challenge ■ The required performance ■ Employee history	
Discussion opening: state purpose of discussion	Pam, the reason that I asked to meet with you today is to discuss your error rate for the past two weeks.
Describe your observations	In reviewing the weekly production reports, I noticed that your percentage of errors has increased by 0.8 percent over the past two weeks. As you know, this is 0.4 percent over our acceptable rate.
Describe your reactions	I was surprised by the information in the reports and am concerned about this trend.
Give the other person an opportunity to respond	What is your view of your error rate?
2. Set expectations: ■ Follow the elements of SMART to clearly outline performance expectations ■ Agree to an action plan	
Discussion	It's important that we establish a clear and measurable plan to address your error rate.
3. Coach and correct: ■ Give the employee direction and support needed	
Discussion	Pam, I know that you're capable of decreasing your error rate to a maximum of 0.4 percent. I'm confident that if you follow the plan we have agreed to, you will achieve your goal.
4. Measure results: ■ Based on the timeline established (set expectations), measure progress and results ■ Determine impact ■ Adjust expectations as appropriate	
Discussion	We'll meet every week to review your progress in relation to the objectives we've set.

POLICY VIOLATION WORKSHEETS AND TEMPLATES

Policy Violation Worksheet 1

Performance challenge	Company dress code
Definition	Employee is violating one or more aspects of the company dress code.
Common reasons for challenge	■ Unaware of the dress code policy ■ Misinterpretation of the policy ■ Disagrees with the policy
Sample SMART objective(s): ■ Specific ■ Measurable ■ Attainable ■ Results-focused ■ Time-based	It's critical that you comply with all components of the company's dress code policy beginning immediately. S: Comply with all components of the policy M: Determine whether or not the employee complies with the policy A: Employee is able to comply with the policy R: Employee is compliant with policy T: Immediately
Keys for leader's success	■ Do not assume that the employee understands and interprets the dress code policy correctly ■ Address the situation in a timely manner ■ Treat the employee and his perspective with respect—manage your nonverbal communication

Policy Violation Template 1

Performance challenge	Company dress code
1. Assess. Describe the following: ■ The performance challenge ■ The impact of the performance challenge ■ The required performance ■ Employee history	
Discussion opening: state purpose of discussion	James, the reason that I asked to meet with you today is to discuss our "casual Friday" dress code.
Describe your observations	The past two Fridays your outfit has not been in compliance with our policy. You wore torn blue jeans and a wrinkled T-shirt.
Describe your reactions	I'm disappointed that I have to discuss this with you. It's important that you comply with our policy.
Give the other person an opportunity to respond	What questions do you have about our "casual Friday" dress code?
2. Set expectations: ■ Follow the elements of SMART to clearly outline performance expectations ■ Agree to an action plan	
Discussion	It's important that you follow the plan we have established and that you clearly understand and comply with our dress code policy.
3. Coach and correct: ■ Give the employee direction and support needed	
Discussion	James, I know that neither of us wants to have this type of conversation again. I'm sure you'll take care of this matter.
4. Measure results: ■ Based on the timeline established (set expectations), measure progress and results ■ Determine impact ■ Adjust expectations as appropriate	
Discussion	We won't need to discuss this again unless you violate the policy in the future. This conversation and our agreed to plan will be in your file. Any additional violations of our dress code policy will result in more serious disciplinary action.

Policy Violation Worksheet 2

Performance challenge	E-mail misuse
Definition	Employee uses the company e-mail program for nonwork purposes or abuses or violates the company's e-mail policy.
Common reasons for challenge	■ Unaware of policy or boundaries of company e-mail use ■ Employee makes an honest mistake
Sample SMART objective(s): ■ Specific ■ Measurable ■ Attainable ■ Results-focused ■ Time-based	Beginning immediately, employee will follow the company's e-mail policy and use her company e-mail address only for appropriate company business purposes. S: Use company e-mail system only for appropriate company business purposes M: Determine, through review of e-mail messages, whether or not the employee complies with the objective A: Once the employee is educated, she has the ability to meet the objective R: Results are in compliance with company policy and expectations T: Immediately
Keys for leader's success	■ Don't assume that the employee understands the company policy or that she understands the boundaries between company and personal e-mail use ■ Be firm ■ Follow up and hold the employee accountable

Policy Violation Template 2

Performance challenge	E-mail misuse
1. Assess. Describe the following: ■ The performance challenge ■ The impact of the performance challenge ■ The required performance ■ Employee history	
Discussion opening: state purpose of discussion	Alex, the reason that I asked to meet with you today is that I have some concerns about your recent use of company e-mail.
Describe your observations	You recently sent a personal e-mail to both coworkers and individuals outside the company that included content that some employees may find offensive. As you are aware, this is against the company e-mail use policy.
Describe your reactions	I understand that it's easy to use our company e-mail to send personal e-mails. However, it's important that you comply with our policy. You put the company and yourself at risk when you use the company e-mail system for personal e-mails with content that is inconsistent with our policies and values.
Give the other person an opportunity to respond	What questions do you have about our company e-mail policy?
2. Set expectations: ■ Follow the elements of SMART to clearly outline performance expectations ■ Agree to an action plan	
Discussion	It's important that you follow the plan we have established. You should clearly understand and comply with our company e-mail policy.
3. Coach and correct: ■ Give the employee direction and support needed	
Discussion	Alex, I appreciate that you're taking this situation seriously, and I'm sure that you will take care of this problem.
4. Measure results: ■ Based on the timeline established (set expectations), measure progress and results ■ Determine impact ■ Adjust expectations as appropriate	
Discussion	We won't need to discuss this again unless you violate the policy in the future. This conversation and our agreed-to plan will be in your file. Any additional violations of our e-mail policy will result in more serious disciplinary action.

Policy Violation Worksheet 3

Performance challenge	Inappropriate use of technology
Definition	Employee uses company technology, such as computer, printer, copier, and e-mail system, for noncompany or inappropriate purposes.
Common reasons for challenge	■ Lack of understanding ■ Employee taking advantage of company resources ■ Lack of personal technology resources
Sample SMART objective(s): ■ Specific ■ Measurable ■ Attainable ■ Results-focused ■ Time-based	Beginning immediately, employee will not use company-owned technology for personal or noncompany purposes. S: Will not use company-owned technology for noncompany purposes M: Monitor whether or not the employee complies with the performance objective A: Once the employee is made aware of the policy, she has the ability to achieve the objective R: Results in employee using company technology appropriately T: Immediately
Keys for leader's success	■ Ask the employee to summarize her understanding of the policy ■ Maintain the employee's self-esteem

Policy Violation Template 3

Performance challenge	Inappropriate use of technology
1. Assess. Describe the following: ■ The performance challenge ■ The impact of the performance challenge ■ The required performance ■ Employee history	
Discussion opening: state purpose of discussion	Connie, I asked to meet with you today to talk with you about a recent issue that has come to my attention regarding your use of your company laptop.
Describe your observations	My understanding is that you allowed your son to use your company laptop to prepare a school project. In addition you took the laptop to school so your son could use it to present his project. This of course is not consistent with our technology policy.
Describe your reactions	I'm upset about your poor judgment. It's important that you comply with our policy.
Give the other person an opportunity to respond	Can you please explain why you allowed your son to use company property?
2. Set expectations: ■ Follow the elements of SMART to clearly outline performance expectations ■ Agree to an action plan	
Discussion	It's important that you follow the plan we have established and that you clearly understand and comply with our company technology policy.
3. Coach and correct: ■ Give the employee direction and support needed	
Discussion	Connie, I can see that you're embarrassed and understand the seriousness of the situation.
4. Measure results: ■ Based on the timeline established (set expectations), measure progress and results ■ Determine impact ■ Adjust expectations as appropriate	
Discussion	We won't need to discuss this again unless you violate the policy in the future. This conversation and our agreed-to plan will be in your file. Any additional violations of our technology policy will result in more serious disciplinary action.

Policy Violation Worksheet 4

Performance challenge	Job abandonment
Definition	Employee leaves the work place or does not report to work without notifying supervisor or other company official.
Common reasons for challenge	■ Illness; not able to contact supervisor ■ Lack of judgment ■ Purposeful
Sample SMART objective(s): ■ Specific ■ Measurable ■ Attainable ■ Results-focused ■ Time-based	In accordance with company policy, the employee will follow the company time-off approval policy and its procedures. The employee must comply with this policy any time he wants or must take time off. S: Employee must follow the company time-off policy M: Determine whether or not the employee complies with the policy A: The employee has the information needed and the ability to meet this objective R: Results will be whether the employee complies with the company policy T: Any time the employee wants time off
Keys for leader's success	■ Ask questions to understand the reason(s) that the employee abandoned his job ■ Clearly communicate that this is unacceptable and cannot be tolerated ■ Ask employee to summarize his understanding of and commitment to the policy

Policy Violation Template 4

Performance challenge	Job abandonment
1. Assess. Describe the following: ■ The performance challenge ■ The impact of the performance challenge ■ The required performance ■ Employee history	
Discussion opening: state purpose of discussion	Michael, I asked you to come in to talk with you about why you left work two hours early without explanation on Wednesday.
Describe your observations	We do not have a request on file for you to leave early, and we did not know where you went. Your behavior is considered job abandonment.
Describe your reactions	I was concerned about you and also frustrated that you had not communicated with me. In addition, your coworkers had to finish a report that you were to submit that afternoon.
Give the other person an opportunity to respond	Why did you leave early without explanation or following our time-off request procedure?
2. Set expectations: ■ Follow the elements of SMART to clearly outline performance expectations ■ Agree to an action plan	
Discussion	It's important that you follow the plan we have established. You must clearly understand and comply with our time-off policy, and you must commit to the communication plan that we have agreed to.
3. Coach and correct: ■ Give the employee direction and support needed	
Discussion	Michael, I appreciate your taking this matter seriously and your commitment to communicating more clearly with me. I'm confident that you won't abandon your job in the future.
4. Measure results: ■ Based on the timeline established (set expectations), measure progress and results ■ Determine impact ■ Adjust expectations as appropriate	
Discussion	We won't need to discuss this again unless you violate the policy in the future. This conversation and our agreed-to plan will be in your file. Any additional violations of our job abandonment policy will result in more serious disciplinary action.

Policy Violation Worksheet 5

Performance challenge	Unacceptable personal hygiene
Definition	Employee does not have acceptable hygiene practices and as a result is offensive to other employees.
Common reasons for challenge	■ Cultural differences ■ Illness ■ Unaware ■ Different definition of hygiene
Sample SMART objective(s): ■ Specific ■ Measurable ■ Attainable ■ Results-focused ■ Time-based	It is important that employee practice basic hygiene so as to not have body odor or other personal hygiene issues that may be offensive to other employees. The employee must improve her hygiene habits immediately. S: Practice basic hygiene habits M: Can measure whether or not employee improves personal hygiene A: The employee has the ability to achieve this objective R: Issue goes away T: Immediately
Keys for leader's success	■ Be direct and clear ■ Check for understanding ■ Take the issue seriously ■ Be compassionate

Policy Violation Template 5

Performance challenge	Unacceptable personal hygiene
1. Assess. Describe the following: ■ The performance challenge ■ The impact of the performance challenge ■ The required performance ■ Employee history	
Discussion opening: state purpose of discussion	Susan, I asked to meet with you today to discuss a personal matter. Lately your level of personal hygiene has been lacking.
Describe your observations	I've noticed that your clothing appears wrinkled and needs to be washed. Your hair is not well-groomed.
Describe your reactions	This is a difficult conversation for both of us. I am concerned about your well-being.
Give the other person an opportunity to respond	Please let me know your thoughts.
2. Set expectations: ■ Follow the elements of SMART to clearly outline performance expectations ■ Agree to an action plan	
Discussion	Your well-being is our first priority. Please take advantage of the resources our company offers to employees to help with personal challenges. It's also important that you address the personal hygiene and grooming issues that we've discussed and outlined in the action plan.
3. Coach and correct: ■ Give the employee direction and support needed	
Discussion	Susan, I know that neither of us wants to have this type of conversation again. However, I would like to meet with you each Monday to see how things are going and to ensure that you're able to execute the elements of our action plan.
4. Measure results: ■ Based on the timeline established (set expectations), measure progress and results ■ Determine impact ■ Adjust expectations as appropriate	
Discussion	We will determine your progress and make any adjustments in our weekly Monday discussions.

Policy Violation Worksheet 6

Performance challenge	Travel and expenses irregularities
Definition	Employee violates one or more requirements of the company travel and expenses policy.
Common reasons for challenge	■ Lack of knowledge about the policy ■ Mathematical error ■ Purposely violates the policy
Sample SMART objective(s): ■ Specific ■ Measurable ■ Attainable ■ Results-focused ■ Time-based	Correct your pending expense report for your recent trip to Boston so that it complies with our travel reimbursement policy. Please have the corrected report to me by the end of the day. S: Correct the expense report so that it is compliant M: The report is corrected or not A: The employee has the knowledge and ability to complete the objective R: Results in a correct expense report, and the employee understands the consequences of making the same mistake in the future T: By the end of the day
Keys for leader's success	■ Be patient ■ Ask employee to summarize her understanding of the travel expense policy ■ Clearly explain the consequences of any further problems on expense reports

Policy Violation Template 6

Performance challenge	Travel and expenses irregularities
1. Assess. Describe the following: ■ The performance challenge ■ The impact of the performance challenge ■ The required performance ■ Employee history	
Discussion opening: state purpose of discussion	Jasmine, I asked to meet with you to review some questions that surfaced regarding the last two expense reports that you submitted to me for approval.
Describe your observations	Both of these expense reports include expenses for dry cleaning. Dry cleaning is allowed, only if the business trip is in excess of three nights. Both of your trips were one or two nights.
Describe your reactions	It's important that I understand everything in the report and that each report be in compliance with the company travel and expense guidelines.
Give the other person an opportunity to respond	Please walk me through your reasoning for including the dry cleaning expenses in your report.
2. Set expectations: ■ Follow the elements of SMART to clearly outline performance expectations ■ Agree to an action plan	
Discussion	It's important that you follow the plan we've established. You must clearly understand and comply with our travel and expense policy.
3. Coach and correct: ■ Give the employee direction and support needed	
Discussion	Jasmine, I appreciate your attention to this matter and trust that you will follow the action plan that we've agreed to.
4. Measure results: ■ Based on the timeline established (set expectations), measure progress and results ■ Determine impact ■ Adjust expectations as appropriate	
Discussion	We won't need to discuss this again unless you violate the policy in the future. This conversation and our agreed-to plan will be in your file. Any additional violations of our travel and expense policy will result in more serious disciplinary action.

ATTENDENCE AND TARDINESS WORKSHEETS AND TEMPLATES

Attendance and Tardiness Worksheet 1

Performance challenge	Excessive tardiness
Definition	Employee is late for work an unacceptable number of times and is violating the company's attendance policy.
Common reasons for challenge	■ Personal challenges ■ Unaware of attendance requirements
Sample SMART objective(s): ■ Specific ■ Measurable ■ Attainable ■ Results-focused ■ Time-based	It is critical that, beginning immediately, employee arrive on time to work each day. S: Arrives to work on time each day M: Employee arrives on time or is tardy A: Employee has the knowledge and ability to achieve objective R: Employee is ready for work on time each day T: Beginning immediately
Keys for leader's success	■ Ask open-ended questions to understand the reasons for tardiness ■ Ask employee to summarize the attendance policy to ensure that the employee understands ■ Clearly outline requirements for being on time for work and the consequences if this does not occur

Attendance and Tardiness Template 1

Performance challenge	Excessive tardiness
1. Assess. Describe the following: ■ The performance challenge ■ The impact of the performance challenge ■ The required performance ■ Employee history	
Discussion opening: state purpose of discussion	Ty, we need to talk about the number of times you've been late to work in the past 30 days.
Describe your observations	You've been between 10 and 20 minutes late four times in the past month.
Describe your reactions	I'm surprised that I have to discuss this with you. As you know, it's important for you to arrive at and be ready to work no later than 8 a.m.
Give the other person an opportunity to respond	Please help me understand why you've been late so often and what you think we can do to address the problem.
2. Set expectations: ■ Follow the elements of SMART to clearly outline performance expectations ■ Agree to an action plan	
Discussion	It's important that you implement the plan we outlined to make sure you get to work on time every day. Do you see any reason you won't be able to follow through on the plan?
3. Coach and correct: ■ Give the employee direction and support needed	
Discussion	Ty, I know that neither of us wants to have a conversation about tardiness again. I know that it can be a challenge to balance our work and personal lives. I'm confident that you'll be able to take care of this problem.
4. Measure results: ■ Based on the timeline established (set expectations), measure progress and results ■ Determine impact ■ Adjust expectations as appropriate	
Discussion	Let's meet two weeks from today to talk about how your plan is working.

Attendance and Tardiness Worksheet 2

Performance challenge	Excessive absence
Definition	Employee is absent from work an unacceptable number of times and is violating the company's attendance policy.
Common reasons for challenge	■ Personal challenges ■ Unaware of attendance expectations
Sample SMART objective(s): ■ Specific ■ Measurable ■ Attainable ■ Results-focused ■ Time-based	To avoid further disciplinary action, it is critical that the employee does not have an unexcused absence from work in the next three months. S: Does not have an unexcused absence from work in the next three months M: The employee either does or does not have unexcused absences in the next three months A: The employee has the knowledge and ability to achieve the objective R: The employee is at work on a regular basis T: Next three months
Keys for leader's success	■ Ask open-ended questions to gain an understanding of why the employee is absent from work ■ Ask employee to summarize the attendance policy so that you can see whether the employee understands it ■ Clearly outline the requirement to be at work and the consequences if this does not occur

Attendance and Tardiness Template 2

Performance challenge	Excessive absence
1. Assess. Describe the following: ■ The performance challenge ■ The impact of the performance challenge ■ The required performance ■ Employee history	
Discussion opening: state purpose of discussion	Anita, we need to talk about the number of times you've been absent from work in the past 60 days.
Describe your observations	You've missed five days in the past two months. This is not acceptable.
Describe your reactions	I'm surprised that I have to discuss this with you. As you know, it's important for you to be at work. Your absence creates more work for your team members, and I am concerned about you.
Give the other person an opportunity to respond	Please help me understand why you've missed so much work.
2. Set expectations: ■ Follow the elements of SMART to clearly outline performance expectations ■ Agree to an action plan	
Discussion	Of course we all miss days periodically because of personal and/or family illness. However, as we agreed, you are expected to be at work each day. Do you see any reason you won't be able to follow through on the plan we agreed to?
3. Coach and correct: ■ Give the employee direction and support needed	
Discussion	Anita, I know that neither of us wants to have a conversation about absences again. I know that it can be a challenge to balance our work and personal lives. I'm confident that you will be able to take care of this issue.
4. Measure results: ■ Based on the timeline established (set expectations), measure progress and results ■ Determine impact ■ Adjust expectations as appropriate	
Discussion	Let's meet two weeks from today to talk about how your plan is working.

Attendance and Tardiness Worksheet 3

Performance challenge	Family Medical Leave Act (FMLA) abuse
Definition	Employee uses the company's Family Medical Leave Act policy to his personal advantage at the expense of the organization.
Common reasons for challenge	■ Does not fully understand the policy ■ Intentionally uses the policy to take extra time off
Sample SMART objective(s): ■ Specific ■ Measurable ■ Attainable ■ Results-focused ■ Time-based	Meet with the benefits coordinator by the end of the week to fully learn about the company FML policy and how to appropriately use the benefit. Further misuse of the policy could result in disciplinary action. S: Fully understand the policy M: Get feedback from benefits coordinator and talk with the employee to measure his knowledge of the policy A: The employee has access to the knowledge he needs to achieve the objective R: The employee becomes knowledgeable and no longer abuses the policy T: By the end of the week
Keys for leader's success	■ Ask open-ended questions to gain an understanding of why the employee is abusing the policy ■ Talk with the benefits coordinator in advance ■ Follow up to ensure that the employee understands the policy and is clear about the consequences if further abuse occurs

Attendance and Tardiness Template 3

Performance challenge	Family Medical Leave Act (FMLA) abuse
1. Assess. Describe the following: ■ The performance challenge ■ The impact of the performance challenge ■ The required performance ■ Employee history	
Discussion opening: state purpose of discussion	Nathan, we need to talk about your most recent application for FML.
Describe your observations	Human resources has asked me to review our family medical leave policy with you to make sure that you understand it. Your current request is not in line with our policy.
Describe your reactions	Of course our policy is there to assist employees with personal issues that take them away from work. However, not all personal issues fall under FML.
Give the other person an opportunity to respond	Please tell me your understanding of the policy and why you believe your current request falls within it.
2. Set expectations: ■ Follow the elements of SMART to clearly outline performance expectations ■ Agree to an action plan	
Discussion	After further review of our FML policy and your request, we both agree that your request does not fall under the policy. You have the option of taking personal or vacation time to address you personal issue.
3. Coach and correct: ■ Give the employee direction and support needed	
Discussion	Nathan, it's very important that you understand and comply with all of our policies, including FML. It's not acceptable to abuse these policies. Doing so will result in disciplinary action.
4. Measure results: ■ Based on the timeline established (set expectations), measure progress and results ■ Determine impact ■ Adjust expectations as appropriate	
Discussion	We will not need to discuss this issue further unless it comes up again.

Chapter 5

How Leaders Can Be Proactive (and Not Reactive) with Performance: Make a Plan and Follow It

How do leaders spend their time? Leaders who take the time to make a plan and implement that plan are typically very successful. They have a clear view of the work that needs to be done and who is and will be doing it. These leaders are also better positioned to adapt to unexpected issues and additional work. They operate in a proactive mode. Other leaders complain that they do not have enough time to be proactive. They do not take the time to make and implement a plan and often spend a significant amount of time in reaction mode. They are pulled in several directions while reacting to each situation as it comes up. They tend to spend a lot of time addressing performance problems and are managed by their work instead of managing their work. These leaders do not have a clear view of work flow and work assignments.

COACHING EMPLOYEES

To successfully manage her team's performance, a leader needs to proactively coach and develop employees. Regular coaching allows a leader to have a clear picture of how well an employee understands her work and projects, as well as her level of performance.

WHAT DOES COACHING MEAN?

Coaching is the interaction between a leader and her team members in which the leader equips team members with the tools, information, and opportunities they need to develop skills and abilities to become more effective. Effective coaches facilitate the success of others by:

1. Understanding the strengths and development needs of each employee as they relate to job performance.
2. Providing each employee with the tools, training, and resources to address his or her development needs.
3. Presenting the employee with opportunities to practice the skills needed to improve.
4. Giving the employee regular feedback about his or her progress.

How much time does a leader need to spend coaching? Research has proven that a leader who spends approximately two hours per forty-hour workweek coaching team members is appropriately investing in the employees' success.

WHAT DOES COACHING LOOK LIKE?

First, it is important to think of coaching as an integral part of day-to-day interactions and not a separate event or meeting. By looking for on-the-job opportunities to coach employees, leaders are making the most of their investment of time and energy. This of course requires the leader to create a plan to interact with team members on a regular basis.

Coaching Strategies

At the end or beginning of each week, make a list of employees and topics that you need to address with them during the upcoming week:

- Schedule time to check in with team members about current projects and assignments.
- Walk through the work area for informal interactions and to observe and be available for questions.
- Make notes during team or project meetings of coaching opportunities that come up during the meetings.
- Reward and recognize team members for improvements.

A small investment of time will have significant return on both the level of performance and the culture of your team.

BACK TO THE PLAN

It is easy to fall into the trap of reacting to the crisis of the day rather than focusing on what is most critical. The first step is to get a better sense of your priorities:

1. List your responsibilities.
2. Rank each responsibility according to importance:

   A = most critical

   B = important

   C = least critical

To help you decide the appropriate ranking for each responsibility, review the results of the in-sync process The Ritz-Carlton uses, which is outlined in Chapter 3. This process outlines the organizational and departmental objectives for which the team is responsible.

Tips for Success

1. Adjust your schedule and priorities as necessary to ensure that your daily work aligns with your most critical job responsibilities.

2. Take the time to talk with team members informally in order to keep in touch with their reactions to work assignments and workload.

3. Periodically repeat this exercise so that the allocation of your time and energy remains in line with your strategy and objectives.

DELEGATION

Now it's time to assign the work—delegate. *Delegation* is the process of sharing authority and accountability with others in making decisions and meeting objectives. Delegation is critical for two reasons:

1. First, as a leader, you are responsible for all the work and output from your area. You cannot accomplish all this work alone.

2. Second, delegating assignments contributes, more than anything else does, to the development of your staff.

Many leaders struggle with effective delegation. They may resist delegating work; they may not know how or feel they should do the work. Common reasons for reluctance to delegate include:

- Lack of time to explain the task or train someone to do it
- Desire for perfection
- Personal satisfaction from completing the work themselves
- Concern with overburdening the team
- Discomfort with team members' performance levels
- Fear of failure

These concerns can be overcome by applying a delegation model:

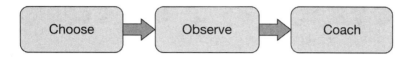

Choose the right employee to carry out the work; match team members to assignments.

Observe the employee's performance. Empower the employee to do the work, monitor her progress, and determine how involved you need to be based on her experience, her level of motivation, and her workload.

Coach the employee through mistakes and questions.

Choosing the right team member to carry out each task is often the most difficult part. It can be easy to assign too much work to your go-to employees and too little to those who require more coaching. However, each team member needs responsibility to challenge his ability. And he should carry his weight on the team. Leaders have the responsibility of not taking the easy way out. They need to delegate to team members who will require more guidance and coaching. This builds skill and confidence in both the leader and the employee.

TEAM ASSESSMENT

To effectively delegate, leaders need to know their team members; what experience they have, what their strengths and weaknesses are, and what motivates each of them. This type of information is invaluable and provides leaders with the foundation for making decisions for assigning work and managing performance.

The following template can be used to gain a clear view of the capabilities of the team and each individual. It can serve as a tool for leaders to review and assess each team member's skill level, as well as the leader's comfort level in delegating tasks to the employee.

Team Assessment Tool

Team Member	Skill Assessment*	Delegation Comfort Level†	Reasons for Comfort Level	Key Contributions to Team
Joe Career	Strong performer	Developing	• Has not spent much time with Joe • Unsure of Joe's analytical skills	Positive attitude

Key:
*Skill assessment:
    A = strong performer
    B = average performer
    C = below-average performer
†Delegation comfort level:
    Strong
    Developing
    Poor
    Nonexistent

To choose the right employees for each task, consider any employee who:

- Has the knowledge or skills to do the work.
- Is interested in the area, or has asked to do similar work.
- Needs to further develop in this particular area.
- Has time to complete the task.

> If you have delegated an assignment and it does not meet your expectations, don't redo it yourself. Explain why it did not meet your expectations and what needs to be changed. Then have the employee redo the work.

Communicate Clear Expectations for Assignments

Without clear expectations employees may waste time or even produce results that completely miss the mark. This is frustrating for both the leader and the employee. Chapter 4 focuses on communication strategies that allow leaders to set clear performance expectations and address issues that may arise.

Empower Team Members to Manage Their Responsibilities

Allowing employees the latitude to carry out their assignments is a key part of effective delegation. Leaders who do not are often seen as micromanagers, and their employees may feel that the leader does not trust them to get the work done. The following strategies can help leaders give their employees enough room to manage their work:

- Ask team members what they need from you to successfully accomplish projects and other assignments. Follow through on their request whenever possible.

- Identify assignments that you can give to your employees that give them full authority.

- Encourage team members to bring solutions along with problems—not just the problem—to give them a stronger sense of responsibility and accountability.

- Try not to strive for perfection. The goal of most delegated assignments should be focused on learning and development and not small, less important details.

Allow employees to move forward with their ideas unless it is too risky. They will learn from the process and any mistakes they make.

COACH

Once the leader has delegated an assignment to the right team member, she now needs to make herself available for questions and direction. This not only helps the employee successfully complete the assignment, but it also lets the leader know how the work is going, what skills the employee is strong at, and what areas he may be struggling with. Leaders can make themselves more available and well-positioned to coach by following these suggestions:

- Keep your calendar up-to-date and share it with your team.

- Meet with team members on a weekly basis, either as a team or one-on-one to review projects, answer questions, and address problems.

- Be flexible when you are traveling or have employees working in different time zones. Schedule calls at times that are convenient for your team members.

- Use informal interactions with employees, such as before or after meetings, to talk about projects and assignments.

- Be visible, keep your door open, and walk around.

MOTIVATION

It is sometimes surprising to leaders that some of their employees are not motivated in the same ways that they are. For example, Steven, a manager of accounts payable, is motivated by deadlines and enjoys working under the pressure of a deadline. He feels that he does

his best work in this type of situation. Because of his own preferences Steven often gives his team members tight or even unrealistic deadlines. As a result his team members become frustrated and
miss deadlines. Steven is also frustrated and does not understand
why these team members do not "rally" to the deadline and deliver
solid performances.

Steven would benefit from taking a step back and gaining a better
understanding of how each of his team members is motivated. Successful leaders gather this information and leverage it as they assign
and manage work. Having the ability to navigate the differences in
each team is critical.

The template on the following page can be used to help leaders
build their understanding of how each employee is motivated and
how to successfully approach each individual.

There are many tools available to help leaders and teams better
understand how each is best motivated. The Myers-Briggs Type Indicator (MBTI) is a validated and easily applied instrument that provides leaders with insight into their own work and communication
style, as well as how others are motivated. Professionally facilitated
team sessions that use a tool such as the MBTI can be extremely
helpful by increasing awareness and removing barriers.

Leaders are not only responsible for understanding how each team
member is best motivated, but they also need to understand how
to modify their own behavior based on that knowledge. The way
the leader communicates tasks, motivates each team member, and
holds each accountable makes the difference between an in-sync,
productive team and one that is out-of-sync. By leveraging the *motivating others* tool, talking with employees about what motivates them,
and observing how they react to different projects, leaders build a
strong database of knowledge about each team member and how to
best achieve team objectives.

The following is a list of different styles and motivations for leaders
and team members:

Driver
- Takes risks
- Pushes oneself
- Achieves stretch goals

Motivating Others

Employee name	
Role	
Communication style	
Learning style	
Overall responsibilities	
Tasks employee does well	
Tasks employee needs to improve	
Strengths to leverage	
Coaching and Developing a Plan	
Best ways to motivate	
Communication approach	**Learning approach**
Notes	

- Puts stress on others
- Wants visible results

Secure and stable

- Prefers stability
- Wants job security
- Likes a predictable schedule
- Seeks a comfortable, clean work area

Balanced

- Is flexible
- Values work-life balance
- Views personal time as a priority

Recognition and control

- Looks for visible assignments
- Focuses on career advancement
- Prefers to take the lead on projects

Independent

- Prefers working independently
- Takes the initiative
- Develops new ideas and processes

Relationships

- Prefers assignments that involve others
- Works for harmony
- Gives to others

Although each person is motivated differently and may prefer specific types of assignments and projects, all employees are responsible for all the work that falls within their purview. Leaders must hold each team member accountable for delivering performance regardless of the team member's preferences. The strategies and resources outlined in Chapter 3 are designed to help leaders hold employees accountable.

Leaders must remember that the focus—what they are holding the team member accountable for—is on results and performance, not the employee's style, which may be very different from the leader's. It may help for the leader to focus on the *what* (result) and not the *how* (the approach or style).

DOCUMENTATION

Sydney is a manager of customer service with five supervisors reporting to her. She has been unhappy with the performance of one her supervisors, Andre. Sydney met with her HR partner, Christina, to talk about her frustrations with Andre and her options for addressing his lack of performance. After Sydney summarized the situation and gave several examples of Andre's performance issues, Christina asked her whether or not she had documented any of the conversations she has had with Andre about his performance and if she had copies of work samples demonstrating the performance problems. Sydney was surprised by this question; she had never thought to document any of her interactions with Andre. Weren't her observations and word enough? Why would she need to keep a record? Andre was clearly not performing at an acceptable level.

Christina explained the purpose and use of documentation.

CLARITY

Although Sydney is very clear about Andre's performance issues, she needs to make sure that Andre clearly understands the issues and what changes he needs to make. Sending a follow-up e-mail that documents the performance conversation ensures that Andre is clear on the issue and agreed-upon action plan. The e-mail serves as documentation and gives both Andre and Sydney the opportunity to address any misunderstandings.

CONSISTENCY

Documenting and keeping a record of key employee interactions help leaders handle performance in a consistent manner. When a performance issue turns into a disciplinary issue, it is critical that leaders use a consistent process and template to document the issue and agreed-upon actions. A lack of consistency can lead to questions of fair treatment. HR partners can provide leaders with a documentation template that is appropriate for the organization. Some key components that should be included are presented below.

COMPLIANCE

Leaders are responsible for being familiar with their organization's employee policies and procedures and how to administer them. Since leaders must manage employee performance problems, they need to do so in a way that is consistent and compliant with the company's policies. Stepping outside of company policies, knowingly or not, can put the leader and the organization in a difficult situation.

PROTECTION

By clearly and consistently documenting performance issues, leaders protect their employees, themselves, and the organization from broader and more complex or even legal issues.

KEY COMPONENTS OF DOCUMENTATION

While each organization's performance plan documents typically have specific and customized components, there are core components that all should include:

- Employee name
- Employee position
- Department
- Date of hire
- Date of performance meeting
- Type of performance communication:
  - ☐ Oral
  - ☐ First written
  - ☐ Second written
  - ☐ Final written
  - ☐ Termination

- Reason for performance communication
- Description of performance issue
- Action plan for improvement
- Employee comments
- Dated signatures

KEEP THESE THINGS IN MIND

It is critical for leaders to keep a few important things in mind when documenting performance conversations and issues:

1. Be purposeful about what you include in performance documentation. Do not include terms or phrases that could be misinterpreted or convey inappropriate messages.

2. Remember that all notes, formal and informal in hard and electronic versions, may be "discoverable" in legal proceedings.

Always have your HR partner review documentation prior to sharing it with the employee.

Chapter 6

30 Starters for Tough Performance Conversations: Waiting and Hoping Won't Cut It

Even the most skilled leaders face those situations in which an employee is underperforming, violating policies, or exhibiting behavior that is not consistent with the company culture. Unfortunately, many leaders are uncomfortable with confronting these situations and choose the "wait and hope" approach to leading, which is "wait and hope the problem gets better and goes away on its own." We all know how successful this approach usually is and how it tends to exaggerate the issues and create even more disruption and conflict in the workplace. It is important to point out that these are recent performance issues that do not represent a disciplinary situation. The purpose of these conversations is to avoid discipline and to instead address the problems before they escalate to a disciplinary status. These conversations may be an entry point into the progressive discipline process that most organizations have in place. These are the tough conversations that leaders have to have with otherwise high- or solid-performing employees. Because of personal relationships, the organization's culture, or a work team's dynamics, these are often the conversations that are avoided or "watered-down," thus resulting in continued and repeated problems or a breakdown of trust between the leader, the employee, and/or the other team members.

YOUR JUST-IN-TIME STARTER KIT

This chapter is designed to clarify for leaders the type of roadblocks they face with their employees and to provide just-in-time starters for the tough conversations they must have. It cannot be overemphasized that these conversations need to take place and that the sooner they happen, the more likely it is that they will lead to the desired results. Too often, while leaders are "gearing themselves up" to have these conversations, the information or situation becomes old and loses relevance in light of other events, decisions, initiatives, and so on. Having the conversation, albeit later than you should, can still be better than not having it at all, but the success rate is much higher if the right conversation takes place at the right time.

FUNDAMENTALS OF MANAGING

This chapter is organized by performance situation. Each section starts by identifying the performance issue or challenge. Issues have been selected to reflect those that are common in many organizations. Next, some context and background are provided for a typical scenario in which the performance issue occurs. The goal is for you to be able to relate to the situation and then be able to adapt and apply it in your own organization. Third, the objective or objectives of each situation is clearly and concisely stated. Learning to prepare a conversation with tangible results in mind is a key ingredient to success. Last, there is a discussion starter that consists of few sentences to get you started on the conversation. Again, this is designed for you to be able to see how the combination of a few key words in each situation can make both the leader and the employee relax, and be open to giving and receiving the feedback in the way it was intended. This approach will consistently and solidly promote the fundamentals of good management.

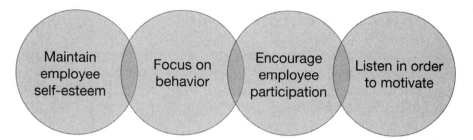

MAINTAIN EMPLOYEE SELF-ESTEEM

Maintaining employee self-esteem is the foundation of the relationship and interactions between leaders and their employees. It is the most important skill that a team leader can master. By definition, it is the ability to assign work, measure and evaluate performance, correct mistakes, and manage and resolve conflicts all while maintaining the employees' sense of dignity and self-worth.

FOCUS ON BEHAVIOR

Leaders who focus on the behaviors or what the employees do, rather than on opinions, emotions, and perceptions, are much more successful in resolving conflict and correcting work habits. This allows both the leader and the employee to see the impact of the behavior and not make judgments based on personal traits or attitudes.

ENCOURAGE EMPLOYEE PARTICIPATION

If leaders are actively involving their employees in real decision making, problem solving, and other nonroutine work activities, they will create an environment of trust and authentic ownership for their teams. This is motivating for both the employees and the team leader.

LISTEN IN ORDER TO MOTIVATE

A leader's ability to listen in a dynamic and active way is critical to the employees' confidence and desire to perform. If employees are validated and positive behaviors are reinforced, they will continue to perform at a high level.

PERFORMANCE CONVERSATIONS

The fundamentals of management are a lot like the auto insurance that we all need to have in order to own and drive a car. Like insurance, the fundamentals are pretty basic, and most people know that they're important even if they don't think about them much. Also insurance is not the sexiest thing, but it's there when you need it, and it usually pays for itself by covering one bad accident. The fundamentals of management will keep you on the straight and narrow, and your successful results will be reinforced each time you put them into action. By using the fundamentals of management as a backdrop, try the following conversation starters to address and resolve your challenging performance conversations.

1. PERFORMANCE CHALLENGE: MANAGING A NEW EMPLOYEE

Typical Scenario

Jessica is a new college graduate hire for the IT department of a large financial institution. She is bright and enthusiastic about her role and anxious to show what she can do. Some of her coworkers, however, have started to complain about how Jessica seems to critique their work and ask a lot of questions about why things are done a certain way. They have started to exclude her from meetings and discussions, and Jessica seems to be frustrated and unhappy.

Objectives

- Understand Jessica's perspective on her new role and team.
- Explain the impact of her behavior on the team.

■ Provide examples of ways to successfully build knowledge and relationships in a new organization.

Conversation Starter

Jessica, you have proven to be a great addition to our team. I really appreciate your enthusiasm and energy, and I want to support you as you continue to learn and transition into your role here. First, I would like to get your perspective on how you feel that you are fitting into the team.

Next, I would like to share some feedback that your team members have given me. They've said that you sometimes overcorrect their work and ask questions that suggest that you don't agree with the process or procedures in place. This causes them to lose trust in you because they feel that you haven't yet learned enough about our organization to make these judgments. Let's talk about some ways that you can ask for the information that you need without creating a perception that you are critiquing someone's work or a process.

2. PERFORMANCE CHALLENGE: CONFLICT(S) BETWEEN TWO EMPLOYEES

Typical Scenario

Mark and Jennifer work together in the accounts payable department and are each responsible for managing invoices from key account vendors. Mark works the first shift, and Jennifer works the second shift. It is important for them to clearly communicate account activity during shift change. They both accuse the other of not sharing key information, which causes rework and confusion.

Objectives

■ Clearly explain the impact their conflict has on the rest of the department and on productivity.

■ Obtain a commitment from Mark and Jennifer to resolve their conflict and work together effectively.

Conversation Starter

Mark and Jennifer, it has come to my attention that the two of you have had difficulty working effectively together over the past month. I'm concerned because this is beginning to have a negative impact on the department and on your individual performance. I thought that the three of us could work this out. What I'd like to do first is to get a clear idea of what the problem is and find a way to solve it. I would like each of you to explain the problem from your point of view. Then the other will explain what you've heard. The first person will confirm the accuracy of the other person's view of the problem. Does this make sense to you?

3. PERFORMANCE CHALLENGE: MISSING DEADLINES

Typical Scenario

Scott has been in his role for 18 months and has been a solid performer. Over the past 2 months Scott has missed three key deadlines.

Objectives

- Understand why Scott is missing deadlines.
- Agree to a plan that will allow Scott to meet his deadlines going forward.

Conversation Starter

Scott, I appreciate your coming in to talk with me today. I've noticed that you've missed a few key deadlines recently, which is unlike you. Can you help me understand why you've missed these deadlines? (List the deadlines if necessary.)

So, it sounds like you've missed your deadlines because . . .

4. PERFORMANCE CHALLENGE: UNACCEPTABLE ERROR RATE

Typical Scenario

Sam works in a distribution center and is responsible for packing orders to be sent to pharmacies and hospitals. The accuracy of all employees is tracked by the merchandise processing system. The system has reported that Sam has a current error rate of 9 percent, 3 percentage points higher than is acceptable, and has been trending downward for the past 30 days.

Objectives

- Understand why Sam's error rate is 9 percent.
- Agree to a plan to improve his rate to 7 percent in the next 21 days and to below 5 percent in the next 45 days.

Conversation Starter

Sam, I've reviewed the department's error rate percentage for the past three weeks, and I noticed that your error rate has been increasing. Let's talk about why and what you can do to improve your error rate.

5. PERFORMANCE CHALLENGE: SUBSTANDARD CUSTOMER SERVICE

Typical Scenario

Peter is a customer service representative for a mobile phone company. He has been in his position for 10 months and is a strong performer. His leader is considering him for a lead position. During a walk through the customer service area yesterday, Peter's leader overheard him talk to a customer with a curt and irritated tone.

When Peter finished the call with the customer, he made a derogatory remark about the call to a coworker. His leader was surprised and disappointed by what he heard.

Objectives

- Ensure that Peter understands that his behavior is unacceptable and that good customer service is essential.
- Gain commitment from Peter that he will handle all customer service calls according to the organization's standards and training.

Conversation Starter

Hi, Peter. Thank you for stopping in to see me. I spent some time in your work area yesterday afternoon at around 2 p.m. and overheard you on a customer call. I have to tell you that I was very disappointed with what I heard. Your tone was curt, and you sounded irritated with our customer. And after you ended the call, I also heard you make a derogatory comment about that customer to Susan. Can you please explain why you handled the call this way?

6. PERFORMANCE CHALLENGE: E-MAIL MISUSE

Typical Scenario

Sarah joined her company as a marketing coordinator 14 months ago. Sarah's leader was part of an e-mail distribution list that Sarah set up to receive e-mails regarding a local issue that was slated to appear on the ballot of an upcoming election. Her leader ignored the first e-mail that he received about three weeks ago, but then he received two additional messages on the same topic this week. The messages are not work-related and clearly represent Sarah's personal opinion on the issue. Sarah's leader is concerned that she is using the company's e-mail system (and identity) as a way to distribute personal mail. This practice is clearly not permitted by the company's e-mail policy.

Objectives

- Help Sarah understand the company policy regarding the use of e-mail for personal communication.
- Stop personal communication using the company e-mail system.

Conversation Starter

Good morning, Sarah. I appreciate your coming in to see me. I need to talk with you about the e-mails you've been sending here at work about [the political issue]. While I applaud your community involvement and passion concerning this, I have to ask that you stop using the company e-mail system to distribute these messages. Are you familiar with our e-mail policy? What questions do you have?

7. PERFORMANCE CHALLENGE: EXCESSIVE ABSENCES

Typical Scenario

Maria is an administrative assistant in a financial services firm and supports three vice presidents. She has been in her role for three years and has been a strong performer. In the past four months, Maria has taken all of her sick days (five) and two weeks of vacation time because of family issues. She has now asked to take three more days of vacation and two personal days next week. Maria's leader has been supportive of Maria; however, her time away from the office is having a negative impact on her work and also creating a great deal of extra responsibility for her coworkers who cover for her. The vice presidents are also not getting the level of support that they require.

Objectives

- Communicate to Maria the impact of her absences on the other administrative assistants and the vice presidents.

- Communicate the need for her to consistently be at work and not miss more days.
- Communicate the decision of her request for additional time off.

Conversation Starter

Hello, Maria. I appreciate your coming in to talk with me. The reason that I asked you to meet with me is to discuss the amount of time that you have been out of the office lately. As we previously discussed, I want to be supportive of your personal situation. Do you agree that we've been flexible in allowing you to use your earned time off?

In the past four months, you've used all your sick days, two full weeks of vacation, and your two personal days. Further absence will continue to put your responsibilities on your coworkers, and the leaders you support will not get what they need. If you need more time to manage your personal situation, we can talk about our leave policy options that may help get you the time that you need and allow us to keep the department running. What are your thoughts?

8. PERFORMANCE CHALLENGE: INAPPROPRIATE LANGUAGE

Typical Scenario

Steve is a leader in a distribution center. He has 15 employees in his department, and he has high productivity numbers as well as high employee satisfaction numbers. Three of his employees, however, have complained about Steve's use of profanity and what they describe as "colorful" language.

Objectives

- Make Steve aware of the complaints and that he is making some of his employees uncomfortable with his language.
- Get Steve to understand that his use of inappropriate language needs to stop immediately.

Conversation Starter

Hi, Steve. How is your day going? Thanks for coming in to meet with me. As I'm sure you know, the latest monthly reports show that your department has once again exceeded its production goals by 2.5 percent. You and your team are doing a fantastic job! I also need to make you aware that it's come to my attention that the colorful language that you use at times is offensive to some members of your team. Are you aware that some of your team members are bothered by your use of profanity?

Steve, it's really important that you know and understand our policy about creating a positive work environment and that you immediately stop using inappropriate language. Do you know what language you use that might be considered offensive? Do you agree to stop using it immediately?

9. PERFORMANCE CHALLENGE: OVERALL PERFORMANCE

Typical Scenario

Mary is a staff accountant at a large hotel chain. She has been in her role for eight months and with the company for three years. Her leader knew that the staff accountant role was a stretch for Mary, and he is now concerned that she is in over her head. Mary has missed three deadlines, has made several serious mistakes on monthly reports, and seems unhappy in her role.

Objectives

- Communicate your assessment of Mary's current performance.
- Determine the next best steps for Mary.

Conversation Starter

Hello, Mary. I appreciate you coming in to talk with me. I think that it's a good time for us to discuss how you're feeling about your new role and for me to give you some feedback. Tell me first how you're feeling about your role and how things are going.

So what I heard is that you . . .

As you know, when I offered you this position, I knew that it would be a stretch assignment for you. After eight months, I have concerns about your ability to do the job. In addition to the missed deadlines and report errors we discussed, you don't seem to be enjoying your job. What are your thoughts?

10. PERFORMANCE CHALLENGE: LACK OF FOLLOW-THROUGH

Typical Scenario

Michael is an engineer in an automotive company. He has been in his current role for fifteen months and with the organization for five years. A key part of Michael's role is to review the mechanical drawings for projects and respond to any issues with the drawings. Michael's leader has received feedback from three project leaders that Michael is turning the drawings in on time; however, he has not followed through on issues raised on drawings. Michael's lack of follow-through is causing more work for the production team once they discover the issues on the drawings.

Objectives

- Give Michael feedback on his lack of follow-through.
- Ensure that Michael understands what is causing the delays and incomplete work.
- Develop a plan to address the need to follow through on issues with drawings to avoid more work for the production team.

Conversation Starter

Hi, Michael. Thanks so much for coming in to talk with me. I know that you are really swamped! How are things going with the Baxter Project? Thanks for the update. It sounds like you're working hard. Michael, I've gotten some feedback regarding your lack of follow-through on drawing issues. Production has received drawings from you that were not correct, and this has caused production delays. Let's walk through your workload and the process you use to review the drawings. Then we can see if we can identify strategies for recognizing issues and your follow-through process.

11. PERFORMANCE CHALLENGE: COMPANY DRESS CODE

Typical Scenario

The Acer Company has a business-casual dress code policy. This policy is clearly outlined in the employee handbook. Kelly, a human resources coordinator has worn a denim skirt that is significantly above her knees and a blouse that is too revealing for the workplace. Kelly's leader has observed her inappropriate outfits and is struggling with how to approach her.

Objectives

- Ensure that Kelly has read and understands the dress code policy and that she complies with it.
- Communicate the message without offending Kelly.

Conversation Starter

Hello, Kelly. How is your day going? Kelly, I asked you in today to review our company dress code policy with you and to let you know that two of the outfits you've worn recently are not in compliance with our policy. Let's look at the policy and review the specifics. [Read actual policy.] Based on the policy, would you agree that the denim skirt and the blue blouse you wore earlier this week are not within our dress code?

I know that this is an uncomfortable topic for you; it is for me too. However, it's really important that we in the HR group are good examples and follow the policies closely. What questions do you have about the dress code policy? Do you agree to dress according to our policy?

Thank you, I appreciate it.

12. PERFORMANCE CHALLENGE: TRAVEL EXPENSE IRREGULARITY

Typical Scenario

Jennifer is a customer service leader for a mid-sized technology services firm. She has been in her current role for three years. Part of Jennifer's role is to meet with key customers on a monthly basis. These meetings often take place over meals. While reviewing Jennifer's most recent expense reports, her leader noticed that she included mileage to and from the restaurant. As a result, her leader audited the last four expense reports that Jennifer submitted and found that she included this expense in all the reports. Her leader knows that she should have caught this error, but she missed it. Jennifer's leader needs to talk with her to explain that mileage to and from restaurants is not a reimbursable expense. They also need to work out how to handle the incorrect reports that were submitted.

Objectives

- Clarify the travel and expense policy with Jennifer.
- Work out a solution for the previously submitted expense reports.

Conversation Starter

Hello, Jennifer. How was your lunch meeting with Mr. Hill from [the client]?

It sounds like you continue to do a great job managing the relationships with our key clients. An issue has come to my attention related to the lunch and dinner meetings that you've had with our clients. I noticed that you included the mileage for these client meetings. This is not a reimbursable expense according to our policy. Were you aware of that?

Let's take a look at the policy and review the specifics. Now that we've looked at the policy, do you understand that mileage is not reimbursable? What other questions do you have?

Now, let's talk through how to deal with your past expense reports.

13. PERFORMANCE CHALLENGE: TALKING INAPPROPRIATELY TO A COWORKER

Typical Scenario

Jim and Henry work together in the logistics department. They have been coworkers for 18 months and have always seemed to have a positive working relationship. Henry met with their leader today about a situation that he recently had with Jim. Henry explained that Jim was working on an assignment that they are both responsible for. Jim said to Henry, "You can really be a lazy &%#!* guy sometimes! I seem to have to do most of the work around here." Henry was upset and startled by this comment from Jim and wanted help from his leader on how to handle it.

Objectives

■ Coach Henry on how to have the conversation with Jim to convey that Jim's comment was out of line and made Henry uncomfortable.

■ Help Henry preserve (and mend) his relationship with Jim.

Conversation Starter

It sounds like you're surprised and upset by Jim's comment to you. Is that right? Is it true that you want to talk with Jim about it, but you don't want to hurt your working relationship?

Let's talk about how to approach Jim and talk to him about what happened and how it affected things. It's important that you communicate your experience to Jim—what you heard and how you felt. Then give him a chance to respond. Once you do this, please come back and talk with me, and we can decide whether or not I need to speak to Jim too. Does that work for you?

14. PERFORMANCE CHALLENGE: UNACCEPTABLE PERSONAL HYGIENE

Typical Scenario

Molly is an accounting leader for a pharmaceutical company. She has been in her role for two and half years and with the organization for six. Molly is a strong performer, and her leader is considering her for a broader role. In the past month, Molly's leader has noticed that her appearance is not polished and professional. More specifically, her hair is not always clean and combed, and her clothing is rumpled and stained with food. Molly has never had this issue before, and her Leader is concerned. She is also nervous about having such a "personal" conversation with Molly.

Objectives

- Find out if Molly is aware that her appearance has changed and find out why it has changed.
- Agree to an action plan to correct the problem.

Conversation Starter

Hello, Molly. Thanks very much for coming in. How is your day going? Molly, the reason that I asked to talk with you is that I am concerned that in the last month or so your appearance has not been as professional and polished as it needs to be. This is an awkward topic to discuss with anyone, but I really feel that it's my responsibility to talk with you about your personal appearance as it relates to the work environment. You have always looked very put together and appropriate in the past, and I've noticed in the last month that your hair looks uncombed, your clothes are a bit rumpled and have some stains, and your breath has been unpleasant. I know that this is a lot to take in and it's uncomfortable. I want to make sure that you are OK, and I want to help address these things in any way I can. Can you help me understand why there has been this change? Let's talk about a plan to address it.

15. PERFORMANCE CHALLENGE: JOB ABANDONMENT

Typical Scenario

Theresa is a receiving clerk in a machine shop. She has been in her job and with the company for six years. Theresa has generally met expectations, but is not necessarily a high performer. Yesterday, Theresa got a personal phone call during her shift and then left for the day without checking first with her leader. She left work two hours before her scheduled shift was over.

Objectives

- Understand why Theresa walked off the job.
- Explain that what she did is classified as "job abandonment" and violates a company policy.
- Explain the consequences of the violation.

Conversation Starter

Hi, Theresa. How are you today? I need to talk with you about your decision to leave work two hours early yesterday without checking with me or anyone else. Please tell me why you left that way. Do you understand that what you did is considered job abandonment and against one of our company's work policies?

16. PERFORMANCE CHALLENGE: SPREADING GOSSIP AND RUMORS

Typical Scenario

Ben runs a call center department with 15 employees. The company has started to outsource some of its call center functions to some southern states. Ben has learned that a few of his team members are telling coworkers and people in other departments that their call center is next and they will all lose their jobs.

Objectives

- Communicate that it is inappropriate to spread this rumor.
- Explain the consequences of spreading the rumor.
- Communicate the expectations and gain commitment that it will stop.

Conversation Starter

Tony, Sam, and Paula, I asked to talk with you about an issue that has come to my attention. I understand that you've been telling some of your coworkers and people in other departments that our department is being outsourced and that everyone is going to lose their jobs. Is that true?

First of all, I'm not clear where that information came from, because as far as I know, it is not true. Do you understand the consequences of creating this type of rumor and gossip? Obviously, people become unnecessarily concerned and distracted from their work. I need you to agree to stop spreading this false information. Do you understand? I promise to communicate to you and your coworkers any news that we receive that would affect our department, our jobs, and the company.

17. PERFORMANCE CHALLENGE: NOT KEEPING YOUR LEADER INFORMED

Typical Situation

Rob is a high-performing financial analyst who was hired out of college to work as a financial analyst at a financial services company. Rob has been in his role for 10 months. Rob is very motivated and regularly makes recommendations for improving processes and reports. Rob's leader has discovered that Rob made changes to a monthly report and has added people to the distribution list.

Objectives

- Explain the importance of informing your leader of changes prior to implementing a change.
- Explain the potential consequences of adding people to the distribution list.
- Agree to a process for implementing changes.

Conversation Starter

Hello, Rob. Thanks very much for coming in to talk with me. As I've told you before, I really appreciate the energy and new thinking that you bring to our team; you've helped us make some key improvements to our processes. I have recently learned that you've implemented a change to the monthly report and also added a few individuals to the distribution list for the report. I was upset when I learned that you did this without discussing it with me. Let's talk through the importance of your informing me about changes you are thinking about making before you implement them, as well as the potential consequences of adding individuals to the distribution list.

18. PERFORMANCE CHALLENGE: MESSY AND DISORGANIZED WORKSTATION

Typical Situation

Mary works as a coordinator in the purchasing department of a large medical center. Part of Mary's role is to track and file hard copies of incoming proposals that respond to the center's official Request for Proposals. Mary's workstation is often cluttered with files, office supplies, and personal items such as empty coffee cups, food wrappers, and water bottles. Mary's leader has asked her informally to clean up her workstation which she did. However, Mary's workstation became cluttered again within two weeks. Mary had difficulty finding a file that her leader asked for yesterday because her workstation is not organized.

Objectives

- Communicate the importance of keeping an organized workstation.
- Ensure that Mary understands the impact of a messy workstation on productivity.
- Agree to a plan for Mary to organize her workstation and keep it organized.

Conversation Starter

Hi, Mary. I appreciate your meeting with me. The reason I asked to meet with you is to talk with you about your workstation. You and I have talked before about the importance of keeping your workstation organized. When I asked you for the Acme file yesterday, you had difficulty finding it. Tell me what you think of your workstation. Help my understand why it's difficult for you to keep your station neat and organized.

You are responsible for handling a lot of paperwork for our team. It's important that you keep your workstation organized so that you or anyone else on the team can access a file when it's needed.

Let's agree to a plan for you to organize your workspace and keep it organized.

19. PERFORMANCE CHALLENGE: TALKING NEGATIVELY ABOUT A COMPANY POLICY

Typical Scenario

Paul has worked for a telecom company in the networking department for 12 years. He has seen a lot of changes to how the company works and the management team during his tenure. The leader of Paul's department has recently announced a change to the department's work schedule. Paul is not happy about the change and how it affects his personal schedule. Paul has been talking with his coworkers and internal customers about the changes and the fact that he does not like them.

Objectives

■ Explain the impact and consequences of talking negatively about company decisions.

■ Gain commitment from Paul that he will stop having these types of conversations.

Conversation Starter

Hello, Paul. Thank you for coming in to talk with me. How are things going on the [name specific project]?

Paul, the reason that I asked to meet with you is that I've observed and have received feedback from others that you have been talking negatively about the change in our work schedule policy. I know that you are well-liked and respected in our department, and I am concerned about the impact your negative conversation about the policy change will have on the department. Can you help me understand why you feel strongly about this policy change?

20. PERFORMANCE CHALLENGE: SAFETY VIOLATION

Typical Scenario

Sam has worked in a pharmaceutical packaging company for five years. Part of Sam's job requires him to wear protective eyewear. Sam's leader has noticed that Sam has not had his eyewear on three times in the last month. His leader has reminded him to put his eyewear on each time.

Objectives

■ Review the safety policy that outlines the requirement for eyewear.

■ Clearly explain the expectations to Sam that he comply with the policy at all times.

■ Follow your company's progressive discipline policy if warranted.

Conversation Starter

Hi, Sam. How are you doing today? Sam, I asked you to meet with me to talk about our policy on wearing protective eyewear. As you know, I reminded you three times recently to put on your eyewear when I saw you out on the floor without it on. Do you understand our safety policy that requires us to wear safety glasses? Let's review it just to make sure it's clear.

Sam, it is critical that you wear your protective eyewear every time you are on the floor for several reasons. First of course is your safety, second is the example you show to other employees, and third is the company's OSHA compliance. Do I have your assurance that you will wear your safety glasses on a regular basis?

21. PERFORMANCE CHALLENGE: HABITS THAT ARE ANNOYING TO OTHERS

Typical Scenario

Joan works as an accounts payable clerk in an office with several other employees. All the employees work in cubicles. Joan has a habit of humming when she is working independently. Three of her coworkers have complained to Joan's leader that her humming is distracting and annoying and that they would like her to stop.

Objectives

- Make Joan aware of her humming habit and its effect on her coworkers.
- Help Joan develop a plan to stop humming at her workstation.

Conversation Starter

Hello, Joan. Thanks for coming in to talk with me. How is your day going?

The reason that I asked to talk with you is to share some feedback about you that I've gotten from some of your coworkers. Are you aware that you hum while you work? Some of us have habits that we're aware of, and sometimes those habits bother people around us. So while I appreciate that you are a positive person and enjoy your work, it's important that you express that in other ways and stop humming while you're at your desk. Let's talk about how you will remind yourself not to hum.

22. PERFORMANCE CHALLENGE: TOO MANY PERSONAL PHONE CALLS

Typical Scenario

Carmen is a claims processor at an insurance company. She has worked in her position for three years and is a good performer. In the past 30 days Carmen's leader has noticed that she is making phone calls a few times each day and that this is affecting her productivity.

Objectives

- Make Carmen aware of the impact her personal phone calls are having on her productivity.
- Gain commitment for Carmen to limit her personal phone calls and get her productivity back to an acceptable level.

Conversation Starter

Hello, Carmen. Thanks for coming in to talk with me today. How is your day going?

Carmen, I need to talk with you about the amount of time I have noticed you are spending on personal phone calls. I understand that all of us need to handle personal matters from time to time while we're at work; however your productivity has decreased as the amount of time you spend on personal matters has increased. Is there something going on at home that is taking more of your time? Can you take care of these phone calls during your lunch break?

It's important that we agree that you will reduce the number of personal calls you are making during work hours to no more than 1 per day and that you increase your productivity back to an acceptable level.

23. PERFORMANCE CHALLENGE: REPEATEDLY DOES NOT FOLLOW PROCEDURES

Typical Scenario

Alex works in a medical billing office for a physician's group. She has been in her job for 18 months. There has been a recent change in how each bill is filed in the billing system, and Alex has repeatedly filed the bills she works on using the old procedure. As a result others who need to access these files cannot locate them.

Objectives

- Explain the impact that not following the procedure has on her coworkers and the process.
- Gain commitment for Alex that she will begin following the procedure immediately.

Discussion Starter

Hi, Alex. Thanks very much for coming in to talk with me today. I appreciate all the extra work that you have been doing lately to get us caught up! I need to talk through the new procedure we introduced last month for filing bills in our updated billing system. When you file a bill using the old procedure, it makes it difficult for your coworkers who need to access the bill to find it in the system; they have to take extra time to backtrack to the old procedure. Help me understand why you are still using the old procedure instead of the new one.

I need you to agree to begin using the new procedure right away. Is there any reason that you can think of that prevents you from doing this?

24. PERFORMANCE CHALLENGE: ANGRY OUTBURSTS

Typical Scenario

John is a sales support employee in a fast-paced consumer products company. He has been in his role for two years and is very good at working with his customers and getting his work done. John is known for his emotional behavior and periodic outbursts when he is under stress. John was angry with a coworker and yelled at him in front of several other people yesterday. The coworker was very embarrassed and is now upset with John.

Objectives

- Clearly explain that this type of behavior is not acceptable and needs to stop immediately.
- Explain the consequences of his behavior on his coworkers and his relationships.

Conversation Starter

John, we need to talk about the incident yesterday when you yelled at your coworker in front of several others. Do you understand that this behavior is unacceptable?

How do you think your coworkers respond and feel when you have an emotional outburst?

As we've discussed in the past, you have strong relationships with our customers, and you do an excellent job getting your work done. However, I've observed that often when you're under stress, you become emotional and yell at your coworkers. As I said, this is not acceptable, and I need you to develop a plan to control your emotions and ensure that these outbursts no longer happen.

25. PERFORMANCE CHALLENGE: FREQUENTLY ABSENT FROM WORK AREA

Typical Scenario

Ron and Jude work together in a distribution center. Their jobs require them to be at their workstation during their entire shift unless they are on a break or at lunch or a team meeting. Of course they are able to use the restroom if they need to by letting their leader know. In the past two months Ron and Jude's leader has been looking for either Ron or Jude, and they have not been in their work area after breaks. When asked where they were, Ron and Jude say they needed to go to the back of the warehouse to get supplies.

Objectives

- To ensure that both Ron and Jude understand that they are required to be at their workstation at all times with the exception of lunch and breaks or with permission from their leader.

Conversation Starter

Ron and Jude, thanks for coming in to talk with me. The reason that I want to talk with you is to discuss the amount of time you are away from your workstations. Over the past two months I've tried to find one of you after lunch or a break four times, and you haven't been at your workstation. Can you help me understand why you are away from your work area for extended periods?

26. PERFORMANCE CHALLENGE: SAYS, "I UNDERSTAND" BUT REALLY DOESN'T

Typical Scenario

Caitlyn was recently promoted to a benefits specialist position from a benefits coordinator. Caitlyn has been in her new role for four months and with the company for three years. Her new role requires her to help the communications department explain employee benefit programs. Caitlyn's leader is concerned that she does not understand some of the benefit programs based on the communications that Caitlyn has written.

Objectives

- Gain an understanding of how well Caitlyn is absorbing her new job training.
- Develop a plan and agreement with Caitlyn for her to demonstrate that she thoroughly understands each benefit program.

Conversation Starter

Hello, Caitlyn. Thanks for coming in to talk with me today, I know that you're very busy. The reason that I wanted to meet with you is to see how you feel your on-the-job training is going. Your new role requires you to have a thorough understanding of our benefit plans. How well do you think you know our benefit programs?

In the last two drafts prepared by our communications department, I had to make several corrections to what you had written. I am concerned that you have not yet learned all that you need to regarding the programs. Let's create a training plan to make sure that you have the resources you need and also a way for me to measure what you have learned.

27. PERFORMANCE CHALLENGE: RESISTANCE TO CHANGE OF A PROCESS

Typical Scenario

Pam has been working as an administrative assistant at her law firm for eight years; she is known as the go-to-person in the firm. Two months ago the firm changed to a new e-mail and calendar software package. Pam was not involved in choosing the new package and is not supportive of the change. Pam has asked to keep using the old system because she does not like the new one. She has not gone to training and is trying to use the fact that she works for one of the key partners to influence and support her case.

Objectives

- Understand why Pam is resistant to the change.
- Work with Pam to address her issues and develop a plan for her to attend training as well as a transition plan from the old to the new software.

Conversation Starter

Hello, Pam. I appreciate your coming in to talk with me today. Thank you for helping me with the board presentation. You did a great job with the graphics. Pam, I need to talk with you about your interest in keeping the old e-mail and calendar software instead of transitioning to the new software. Please help me understand your resistance.

It's important that you become familiar with the new system and begin to use it. We're not able to allow you to continue to use the old system so you will need to make the transition. Please create a plan with a timeline for you to learn and implement the new software.

28. PERFORMANCE CHALLENGE: MAY BE UNDER THE INFLUENCE ON THE JOB

Typical Scenario

Seth works in the admitting department of a large hospital; he has been in this role for 18 months and has been a solid performer. A coworker has noticed that the past two Fridays, Seth has returned from lunch with a smell similar to alcohol on his breath and his mood is sullen. The coworker has spoken with their leader about her observation.

Objectives

- Express concern and share the observations with Seth and inform him of resources available to him at the hospital.

Conversation Starter

Hello, Seth. How are things going today? I saw that we have had a high number of admissions today.

Seth, I wanted to talk with you about a more personal topic. I'm concerned about some specific behavior that others have observed after you returned from lunch on two occasions. Your breath smelled similar to alcohol and your mood was sullen on these occasions. Seth, you are a valued member of our team, and I want to make sure you are aware that, if you need them, the hospital has very good resources through our employee assistance program for employees dealing with a variety of issues. I'm going to leave a brochure with you about the program; it is completely up to you whether or not you use it. Please let me know if you have any questions that I can help you with. You also need to understand that it is unacceptable and against hospital policy to be under the influence of drugs or alcohol at work. If this should happen again, there will be serious consequences, and I will have to enforce our disciplinary policy. Suspension or termination could result.

29. PERFORMANCE CHALLENGE: COMES TO MEETINGS UNPREPARED

Typical Scenario

Stacey is a marketing coordinator at a technology firm. She has been in her role for two years. Stacey's role requires her to track all current marketing programs and report on their status at weekly meetings. Stacey's reports have not been current for the past three weeks. Stacey's leader talked with her after the second time the reports were not up-to-date.

Objectives

- Understand why Stacey has not been updating the reports.
- Have Stacey develop a plan to ensure that her reports are current for the weekly meeting.

Conversation Starter

Stacey, can you please walk with me to my office after the meeting. I would like to talk with you for a few minutes. Based on our conversation last week, I expected that your weekly report would be up-to-date for today's meeting. I was very surprised that it wasn't. Help me understand why your report was not up-to-date.

In order for us to effectively manage all our projects, it's critical for the weekly reports to be accurate. Please outline a plan to get back on track and be prepared to review your plan with me tomorrow morning at 8 a.m. Include any support or resources you need from me or anyone else. Do you have any questions?

30. PERFORMANCE CHALLENGE: REGULARLY INTERRUPTS—DOES NOT LISTEN

Typical Scenario

Dave is an analyst in the IT department at an insurance company. Dave has very strong technical skills and can often solve systems issues that others cannot. His leader has noticed that when Dave is speaking with his internal customers, he often interrupts them and talks over them. As a result he does not gather all the information he needs to solve the problem. In addition he is developing a reputation for being a know-it-all, and some internal customers have asked to have a different analyst work on their projects.

Objectives

- Help Dave understand the importance of active listening for his technical projects and his relationships and reputation in the organization.

Conversation Starter

Hello, Dave. Thank you for coming in to see me. Great job handling the systems issue in the claims group, I know the team really appreciates your work.

Dave, I need to talk with about a nontechnical challenge. As you know, in addition to being technically strong, it is also critical for you and our other analysts to have strong communication and listening skills. I've received feedback from both your coworkers and your internal customers that you don't have strong active listening skills. How do you react to this feedback? Let me give you an example. Do you remember when you were working with the property and casualty team to build a new database to track their claims? The team leader was very pleased with your outcome; however, she came to me to let me know that the project took 7 to 10 days longer than it should have because you didn't listen to what their needs were before you designed a solution. So your design had to be reworked once you better understood their needs. In addition, you blamed the team members for not clearly explaining their needs. What are your thoughts about this feedback?

10 CONVERSATION STARTERS FOR LEADERSHIP PERFORMANCE CHALLENGES

If I accept you as you are, I will make you worse; however, if I treat you as though you are what you are capable of becoming, I help you become that.

Johann Wolfgang von Goethe, German poet (1749–1832)

Often senior-level leaders face performance challenges from their direct reports who are also leaders in the organization. Sometimes, these situations can have more serious implications to the organization and affect more individuals or teams. These conversations can be more difficult for leaders to have because of the complexity of the situation, the past history with these individuals, the political landscape, or the current state of the relationships within the leadership team. However, it is no less important, and usually critical, that these issues are addressed as swiftly and appropriately as possible to minimize disruption to the organization and to get the leader back on track.

Leadership Performance Challenges

1. Not delivering results
2. Did not complete performance reviews on time
3. Does not communicate key company information to the team
4. Gives feedback inappropriately
5. Does not give clear direction
6. Does not hold employees accountable
7. Shows favoritism
8. Makes bad decisions
9. Cannot make decisions
10. Poor presenter

TIPS FOR SUCCESS

Here's how to manage your nonverbal communications.

The Most Important Nonverbal Cues	
Eye contact	The visual sense is dominant for most people and therefore especially important in nonverbal communication. *Is this source of communication missing, too intense, or just right?*
Facial expression	Universal facial expressions signify anger, fear, sadness, joy, and disgust. *What is the face you show? Is it masklike and unexpressive, or emotionally present and filled with interest?*
Tone of voice	The sound of your voice conveys your moment-to-moment emotional experience. *What is the resonant sound of your voice? Does your voice project warmth, confidence, and delight, or is it strained and blocked?*

Posture	Your posture—including the pose, stance, and bearing of the way you sit, slouch, stand, lean, bend, hold, and move your body in space—affects the way people perceive you. *Does your body look stiff and immobile, or relaxed? Are your shoulders tense and raised, or slightly sloped? Is your abdomen tight, or is there a little roundness to your belly that indicates your breathing is relaxed?*
Touch	Finger pressure, grip, and hugs should feel good to you and the other person. What "feels good" is relative. Some prefer strong pressure; others prefer light pressure. *Do you know the difference between what you like and what other people like?*
Intensity	A reflection of the amount of energy you project is considered your intensity. Again, this has as much to do with what feels good to the other person as what you personally prefer. *Are you flat or so cool that you seem disinterested, or are you over the top and melodramatic?*
Timing and pace	Your ability to be a good listener and communicate interest and involvement is affected by timing and pace. *What happens when someone you care about makes an important statement? Does a response—not necessarily verbal—come too quickly or too slowly? Is there an easy flow of information back and forth?*
Sounds that convey understanding	Sounds such as "ahhh, ummm, ohhh" uttered with congruent eye and facial gestures communicate understanding and emotional connection. More than words, these sounds are the language of interest, understanding, and compassion. *Do you indicate with sincere utterances that you are attentive to the other person?*

Together, these nonverbal signals communicate your interest and investment in others. Critically important is the fact that these elements are experienced much more intensely in the pauses between words. Interruptions in the flow of language offer us the best opportunities for emotional communication. How well you are able to navigate pauses and send these signals will depend on your ability to manage stress and experience your own emotions as well as those of the other person.

USE THE 60-SECOND RULE

Do not talk for more than 60 seconds before asking the other person for input. The discussion starters included in this book are designed with the 60-second rule in mind.

Consequences of not adhering to the 60-second rule may include:

- You are not able to confirm whether the other person under-stands your message.
- You do not gain important feedback from the other person that will help you adjust your message if necessary.
- You "lose" the other person; he or she will begin to lose focus on your message and start to think about:
    - □ "What is she talking about? I don't do that!"
    - □ "I wonder who told him about this."
    - □ "I have three reasons why she is wrong."

The 60-second rule helps you and the other person to stay focused on your message and allows you to ask for important input to ensure that you are communicating the message you intended.

KEY CHAPTER TAKEAWAYS

This chapter gives leaders practical, actionable strategies for addressing a wide range of performance issues. By using the tem-plates and tools outlined, leaders are equipped to both manage the issues and build strong relationships with their team members.

- Address performance issues as they occur—do not use the "wait and hope" method.
- Keep the fundamentals of management (maintain self-esteem, focus on behavior, encourage participation, and listen in order to motivate) as a backdrop for all performance conversations.

Chapter 7

Managing Performance in Today's Dynamic Workplace

Today's workplace requires leaders to manage performance in a kind of dynamic environment their predecessors did not encounter. This chapter focuses on three dynamics that current leaders need to understand and successfully navigate as they lead their teams and manage performance:

1. Workplace drama
2. Multiple generations in the workplace
3. Long-distance employees

ARE YOU HANDLING THE DRAMA?

As a leader, do you ever feel that you are shoveling coal in the boiler room instead of navigating the ship? Do you find yourself caught in the drama of power struggles, gossip, backstabbing, and manipulation?

By the time you realize you have employee performance problems, your organization may already be misdirected, sinking, plagued by dysfunction, battered by hail, and unable to make progress toward its goals. In some cases, the goals themselves may get lost or diluted amidst the dysfunction.

Marlene Chism, speaker and author of *Stop Workplace Drama* (Wiley, 2011), calls this dysfunction that keeps us from our best, "drama." "Drama is any obstacle to our peace or prosperity," states Chism. No matter what the symptoms—absenteeism, turnover, office politics—the root is always drama. Drama spreads like the flu throughout an organization and eventually hits even the clients and customers who come through the lobby door. Drama hampers productivity and reduces profits. What if you could proactively avoid the storms, leaks, and fog? What if you could align your team members with the mission of the organization and engage them in such a way that they were equipped to avoid dysfunction and were instead motivated to achieve greatness? What incredible things would happen if you were able to shine a light for your employees so that they could navigate the drama and row straight to your island destination?

THE LANGUAGE OF THE ISLAND

Chism uses what she calls "the language of the island" to help teams creatively address performance problems and create a nonthreatening visual impression. As Chism teaches, "Once the team learns how to communicate in a state of non-attachment, the solution often appears. Once you eliminate the blaming, defending or justifying, employees use the power of creativity to look objectively at what is happening."

For example, when a company is allocating dollars to the top line but losing money through turnover, Chism would invite the management team to visualize a leak in the boat to represent the real problem: "Companies will invest hundreds of thousands of dollars on a new system or more sales people instead of addressing the real problem that is losing the company money—which is often a component of drama. You can blame the boat maker, you can complain about the leak, and you can purchase a new motor, but until the leak is plugged, you will still have a sinking vessel."

Using her powerful "stop your drama" methodology for solving employee performance problems, Chism offers eight universal principles and problem-solving tools that work as an integrated system to help you plug the leaks, clear the fog, and get your team rowing together in unison instead of beating each other with the oars.

CHISM'S EMPLOYEE PERFORMANCE PROBLEM-SOLVING TOOL KIT

The following tool kit gives leaders practical strategies and resources to effectively manage employee drama.

1. Clarity

Chism states, "The one with clarity navigates the ship, and everyone else shovels coal." In all drama, there is always a lack of clarity. Either what you are doing doesn't go along with your stated company goals or your own values, or you're not communicating clearly. When you are off mission, everyone is confused and grasping for control. Very few people can function optimally for a company or manager who lacks integrity.

Gaining clarity is the first step toward eliminating and preventing drama. Achieving clarity involves becoming aware of your own values, the mission of the organization, and your role as it relates to everyone else. You must know where you are, who you are, and where you want to go in order to know how and where to lead your employees.

Your values guide you in how you lead. If you act against your values or those of the organization, your efforts will fail. They are like the heart beating in your chest; you don't have to be conscious of them moment to moment, but you need them to be there, providing you with nourishment and life in all you do.

Are you acting on your goals and values? You are applying your management and leadership toward the mission of the organization, or you are not. If you aren't yet clear, take some time to think about what it is you want from your life and your company. Align yourself.

Next, create tools to support your clarity. You may need to create evidence or reminders of your goals. Other clarity tools that we often don't recognize are our written policies, employee handbooks, and standard operating procedures. If you put thought into creating these documents, or if you reference them in times of doubt, you will have better odds of navigating the fog.

Clarity also involves consistency in enforcing the rules. Don't toss around conflicting messages. When a manager has a favorite employee and lets her break the rules, it creates fog. Or if you get angry at an employee the fifteenth time he comes in late, but you have never corrected him before, then you are equally to blame for the problem. You need to speak up quickly, to correct performance issues, and prevent them from repeating themselves. Yes, he was out of line, but you let it happen.

The rules are there for a reason—to keep everyone in agreement. If the rules and procedures are not working anymore, then spend the time to adjust them, says Chism.

2. Identify the Gap

Imagine that you know you want to go to Island A, but you are in the middle of the ocean. There are miles of vast sea yet to travel. This is the gap. The gap is the distance between where you are and where you want to be. Managing the gap requires setting realistic expectations and providing the necessary resources for the team to accomplish the tasks at hand, emphasizes Chism.

Almost any change initially looks easier than it really is. Any time you tackle a significant shift, whether it be a merger, software upgrade, or reorganization, you have to not only engage in regular communications, but you also must be realistic about the resources needed, potential difficulties, and real possibility of facing a shark somewhere on the journey. If you put unrealistic demands on your team and members are not aware of what will happen, they may become very reactive. If your team members know in advance that they are going to have to do extra work, they can adjust, and in fact, might be more engaged to pitch in during the transition. Always communicate and be realistic about the gap and be willing to hear under what circumstances your employees are having trouble. Your employees can usually sense if there is change or drama ahead whether you mention it or not, so being honest and forthright will help reassure them, give them the opportunity to create solutions, and keep them in the boat with you.

3. Telling the Truth

Chism reminds us that telling the truth requires separating facts from thoughts and feelings. What is really going on rather than what do you feel about what is going on?

When you get into conversations such as, "Well she did this, and it's not fair," productivity drains out of your boat. If you spend one hour a week gossiping or complaining, and multiply that by three people, you lose thousands of dollars per year in wages for the time spent. If it were just one person complaining, it would be fine; but negativity spreads like a virus.

In a conversation with Vicki Suitor of Suitor Financial, she said, "Manage the results, not the conversation." This requires applying clarity in your communications, and listening and speaking toward the end result, rather than getting caught in the drama of the emotion and replicating it through gossip or negativity.

One way to incorporate a "telling the truth" policy is to hold regular meetings in order to keep the communication alive. Ask employees to come to you with a solution to each problem they see. This will get them looking beyond the complaint, looking at the actual truth of what is before them, while brainstorming a solution. It will prevent the need to gossip and complain. And it will teach them to become creators, rather than victims.

4. Reinvent and Realign

Even when you have clarity about where you want to go, your boat can be struck by a storm and get temporarily knocked off course. Or, maybe as you row toward the island, you learn new information that alters your course slightly, and you get stuck on a rock called "how." A healthy manager will recognize these pitfalls along the way and be open to applying the best of what is learned in the process.

Expect these pitfalls to occur. Norman Vincent Peale said, "The only people I have ever known to have no problems are in a cemetery." Strong leaders motivate their employees through setbacks by learning from challenges and then using that experience as fuel.

Reinventing and realigning after a setback involves asking, "Where do we need to shift gears? Where have we gotten off track?" It involves recognizing whether you can state, "Our mission is so long and drawn out that it is not inspiring."

Reinventing and realigning is necessary so that you adjust to today's economy and problems. In that way, since change is always around the corner, you are always in a sense reinventing. Whether it's about improving your communication skills or something else, this stage is about continuous growth. Being in a constant state of awareness as to how you can reinvent and realign will cause you to proactively avoid the dangers of being caught unprepared.

5. Stop Relationship Drama

All drama has a relationship component. Relationships exist first on the level of thinking. In other words, how you "think" about your employees has an impact on their performance and on their teamwork. Employees live up to the expectations you have of them. So as a leader, if you want someone to change, you first have to ask, "How do I see my employees?" If you see them as valuable or capable of handling your truth, you'll have conversations that are in alignment. If you see people through the lens of, "Well, she's always been a troublemaker," or "If I get onto her, she'll get all dramatic," then your communication will be full of that energy as well. If you instead see people as responsible creators, your communication will follow.

One of the best tools to help you recognize dysfunction in relationships is the Karpman drama triangle, which illustrates three dysfunctional patterns always present in drama: victim, rescuer, and persecutor. The victim feels hopeless, the rescuer takes on issues that are not his or hers to own, and the persecutor is the one beating everyone in the boat with the oars.

While some leaders are persecutors and have trouble managing their tempers or are too harsh, most managers immediately see themselves as rescuers. An example is avoiding a much needed conversation to "save feelings," or to hide information from the senior executive in order to avoid some unwanted repercussion. How often do managers let one poor performing employee get by without correction only to move to another department and leave another

The Karpman Drama Triangle—Three Patterns—
Victim, Rescuer, and Persecutor

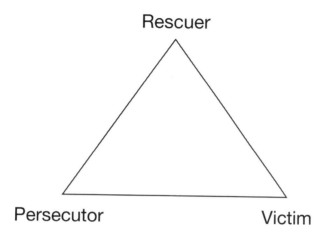

unsuspecting manager with the problem? This doesn't create a good situation and is not fair to the new supervisor or the employee.

Although the initial intention behind rescuing is to smooth things over, eventually rescuing leads to drama and dysfunction. The helpless employee always has an excuse for poor performance. We can call this excuse "the story." When you rescue, it is as if you are hooked onto the story instead of expecting more from the employee.

You must quit honoring the "story" and instead honor the person enough to be honest and help her develop to her potential. Every time you rescue, you reinforce the victim mentality.

On the other hand, if you allow bullying from an employee or a leader, you must own the part you play and stop permitting a persecutor to contaminate the workplace.

6. Master Your Energy

There are five kinds of energy: physical, mental, emotional, spiritual, and environmental. Mastering your energy requires taking personal responsibility—getting the rest you need, taking your own breaks, knowing yourself. All these types of energy interact with each other. We have to know that we may get cranky and snippy with each other, but we need to really try to balance our energy. It's about your own energy mastery.

This also means practicing emotional management. If you are leading from a place where you easily have temper outbursts, you will be causing a chain reaction among your employees that will cause, not prevent, problems. Imagine a boss who yells like a grumpy toddler when things don't go his way. Does this motivate employees to do their best, respect the leader, or even listen? Probably not. Speak your truth, but speak it clearly and be in control.

7. Release Resistance

All drama has a component of resistance. Resistance is the nonacceptance of what is and an unwillingness to consider the available choices for change. Resistance is like saying, "There's a leak in the boat. Someone is going to pay for this. I can't believe this is happening to me. This is not fair."

Releasing resistance means saying instead, "There's a leak in the boat. I don't like it; but I must first accept it. Then when I accept it, I can decide what the next step is."

In the first scenario, time is wasted complaining. In the second situation, there is acceptance of what is, and the mind is freed to consider the next right step. As long as there is resistance, there is wasted time and energy. Releasing resistance is about becoming fully responsible for the outcome instead of using complaints, excuses, and regrets as a distraction to getting the job done.

8. Become a Creator

Open the field of possibilities. When things are not going the way you want, instead of brushing things under the rug, ask how you can engage your team members. How can you get their input? Because if you think you are the only one capable of creating a change, you will have a lot of problems. When you start profiling people, saying, "Sally is the expert on databasing, so when we make this change, we want Sally to do this," we are making Sally feel important and giving her ownership, so that she is rowing with the team. Even in customer service, rather than always correcting your staff, start to get their opinions about how to handle problems or even good experiences, because once they start teaching positive behaviors and recognizing them in each other, they will start noticing and acting on them.

Row to the island called "improving customer service," instead of rowing to the island called, "What did everyone else do wrong?" In other words, you will naturally go in the direction of your strongest intention, so make sure you know what outcome you desire before you take action. Committing to regular meetings will help you state your intentions and measure your results.

According to Chism, you have to be the one solving the customer service problem instead of proving that you were right. You can do this by holding meetings and creating the type of customer service that your customers would want.

A PROACTIVE BOAT

If you can practice the eight steps discussed above and include them as part of a solving employee performance tool kit, you are more apt to proactively avoid fog, distractions, storms, and glittery casino-laden islands along the way. You are more apt to have the skills you need to navigate reefs and unexpected gales. And you are more apt to reach that island with all your employees onboard, where you can sip the coconut juice and frolic in your success.

For more helpful ways on how to put an end to employee gossip, power struggles, poor team coordination, and other workplace dramas that get in the way of productive employee performance, visit Chism's Web site, www.StopWorkplaceDrama.com, today.

MANAGING MULTIPLE GENERATIONS IN THE WORKPLACE

The second dynamic that current leaders need to navigate through involves the multigenerational workplace. Here we focus our attention on Mark, a 38-year-old director of accounting in a mid-sized technology firm, who has a team of six managers. Mark is proud of his education and the relatively fast track he took to the director level. He also prides himself on keeping up on new business and technology developments and teaches himself how to use and integrate new tools into both his work and personal life. While Mark works hard, he also highly values his personal time and sees the world as wide open with lots of opportunities available.

Mark has found that not all of his managers view the workplace and their career in the same way that he does. Initially this frustrated him, and he based part of his performance assessments on these differences. However, Mark has figured out that he can be much more successful and also have a more cohesive team if he "meets each of his managers where they are" instead of expecting them to convert to his way of thinking and working.

For the first time in history the workplace is a mixture of employees from (at least) four generations. Each generation brings its unique approaches and definitions to work, different ideas of how performance should be evaluated, and different expectations of both its leader and the organization.

Leaders need to have a high level of awareness of each generation and understand how to manage the performance of employees within each. Ignoring the differences that each group brings and attempting to use a "one size fits all" approach is certain to result in performance, morale, and cultural challenges. Leaders who embrace the diversity of a multigeneration team create a rich, dynamic, and high-performing group.

While there are numerous terms, years of birth, and descriptions, there are four generations that are most commonly recognized:

1. Traditionalists
2. Baby boomers
3. Gen Xers
4. Gen Yers

Following is a definition and list of core characteristics for each that gives leaders a guide for both motivating and managing the performance of each generation.

Generation	Birth Years	Characteristics	Keys for Success	Notes
Traditionalists	1927–1945	• Practical • Loyal • Hard working • Respects authority	• Secure work environment • Take a personal approach • Show that you recognize their hard work	• 90 percent have retired • Often serve as company historian
Baby boomers	1946–1964	• Work-centric • Independent • Status-focused • Self-centered	• Publicly reward accomplishments • Get consensus • Acknowledge work ethic • Ask to share knowledge	• Nearly 80 million plan to leave the workforce in next decade • Several may have to stay in the workplace because of economic conditions
Gen Xer	1965–1980	• Flexible • Technology savvy • Impatient • Look for "family" in the workplace	• Up-to-date tools • Acknowledge outside interests and time to pursue them • Assign projects and allow workers to independently manage them	• Smaller group than previous and succeeding generations • Highly educated • Ethnically diverse
Gen Yer	1981–1995	• Optimistic • Team-oriented • Committed to social responsibility • Disagreeable and demanding	• Create a team approach • Give opportunities to increase skills and add to education • Create an even playing field	• Fastest-growing segment of the workforce • Largest available workforce • Frustrated by current job market

MANAGING PERFORMANCE RELATIONSHIPS AMONG LONG-DISTANCE EMPLOYEES

Miranda is responsible for a very important, highly visible project in an Asian-based automotive company. She works from the company's North American headquarters and has six team members—two also work at the NA headquarters, two in different states, one in Asia, and one in Europe. Miranda was a very successful project manager prior to this assignment; however, all of her team members were in the same location in her previous role. She has worked hard to set up a communication structure that allows her to keep in touch with each of her team members, as well as foster communication and a sense of team among them.

The third workplace dynamic, managing long-distance performance relationships and challenges among employees is becoming more and more common and complex. Technology, labor pools, and demands of Gen X and Y employees have created a more geographically dispersed workforce. Leaders such as Miranda need to be excellent communicators and cannot afford to be reactive.

Typical challenges of managing long-distance performance relationships include:

- Time-zone differences
- Logistical issues
- Employees who work from home offices
- Regional differences within the same country or state
- Keeping track of performance

Leaders need to clearly identify which of these factors are "at work" in their team and then create a plan to address each and stay in a proactive mode.

The following strategies will assist leaders with many of the challenges of managing issues and relationships between long-distance team members.

- Clearly outline a meeting architecture and communicate it to the team:
  - □ Standing calls and visits

   □ Standard agenda and template for updating assignments and projects

   □ Clear roles and responsibilities for each interaction

- Commit to as much oral and face-to-face communication as possible. Use e-mail for confirming and sharing documents.

- Use technology such as videoconferencing and Skype for one-on-one and team meetings.

- Create (openly) feedback loops with key partners, such as peers and internal or external customers who are in the same location as team members.

- Stay committed to your communication plan; adjust to your team members' time zones whenever possible.

- Use regular reporting and other technology tools, as well as interactions to get the full picture for evaluating performance.

- Avoid e-mail as a vehicle for discussing performance.

Managing performance of employees who live and work in a different location can be tricky, and, if not managed correctly and effectively, can create issues that may not surface for quite some time. Here are dos and don'ts that will set the leader up for success.

Dos and Don'ts of Managing Performance Long Distance	
Do	**Don't**
Address performance issues as soon as they surface	Let the issue go because of distance
Talk in person about serious performance issues	Completely rely on input and information from third parties
Ask a lot of open-ended questions to gain information and understanding	Abandon the employee
Listen to your gut	Have performance conversations:
Manage your nonverbal communication and observe the nonverbal communication of the employee	• In the car • Rushing to a meeting • Boarding an airplane • When you cannot focus

The need to manage the performance of a long-distance team will continue to increase. There are significant benefits including efficiency, cost savings, and ability to hire team members with the best skill set, regardless of their location. Organizations and leaders who create such teams need to commit to building and implementing a clear communication strategy that sets the teams up for success and keeps members connected to one another and the overall organization. Leaders who are purposeful and leverage the strategies and resources provided in this and previous chapters will see a high return on their investment.

Chapter 8

Coach and Develop: Case Studies, Templates, and Tools

Stephanie Montanez has been called one of California's HR thought leaders, as well as a subject-matter expert in improving employee performance through a wide variety of tried-and-true methods. Her philosophy is to improve performance and avoid employee performance hurdles by using a "praise in progress" methodology and a "direct and specific feedback" methodology, along with effective formal "employee coaching and development plans."

Formerly an HR professional with Qualex, a wholly owned subsidiary of Kodak, Montanez now heads up the human resources division of MedAmerica's Medical Billing Services, Inc. (MBSI), as its director, in Northern California. She also created MBSI's employee development and coaching division, with locations throughout California and Arizona.

Currently Montanez is the executive producer and the voice and face of HumanResourcesSources.org and its highly popular internal media programming channel, along with the HumanResources Sources.org Web site, where tips, tools, and cutting-edge HR techniques can be found in interviews, teleseminars, Webinars, tool kits, TV programs, MP3 downloads, and podcasts, broadcasted continually and at HR conference settings around the world.

EMPLOYEE PERFORMANCE TOOL KIT: SEVEN EASY STEPS TO FAST, EFFECTIVE, AND ACTIONABLE EMPLOYEE PERFORMANCE IMPROVEMENT

Some of Montanez's critical steps to improving employee performance are outlined below. Each step provides an activation process for her sample templates, which are provided in this chapter. The following includes an interview with Montanez conducted during an HR event where she was speaking.

STEP 1   The first step is evaluating and diagnosing the deficiency to determine a positive action plan for improvement. Until you diagnose the problem, you cannot assist the employee in improving performance. Many times the deficiency is training, proper equipment, or computer programs. Sometimes the employees lack the ability to perform the essential functions of the position.

STEP 2   Discuss the deficiency with employees and ask for their assistance in improving their performance. Ask them what you can do as a leader to provide them with the proper training and tools they need to be successful. By asking employees for assistance in this, you are getting their buy-in on the improvement plan and feedback on their particular learning style.

STEP 3   Draft an employee coaching and development plan to address the deficiencies and provide a comprehensive action plan for improvement. By doing this, the employee is aware of the deficiency and has a written plan for improvement so that he or she knows what is needed to be successful.

STEP 4   During discussion of the employee coaching and development plan, provide praise and positive reinforcement for all goals that were achieved and use the "soft sandwich" approach when providing negative feedback. The soft sandwich approach is, "Give them positive feedback, then give them the negative feedback, and then give them positive feedback." This way the coaching sessions end with a positive tone. If employees feel that they are improving and believe that they can improve, they usually will.

STEP 5 If employees fail to meet the required expectation, move on to the next step of the employee coaching and development plan. Have another conversation with them and ask for any additional items or tasks that they need assistance with. Once this is completed, draft a formal coaching plan for improvement. Provide additional training during this time, ask the employees to go to their supervisor for additional questions, cheat sheets, and job- or task-specific training. At this point the employees' leaders should set time in their schedule to have regular meetings with employees to address any questions that they might have. The employees can have a folder to place all questions, and the leader can meet with them daily at a specific time to answer any questions. The leaders should also have the employees write down any questions that they have. When the leader answers the question, the employees write down the answer. At that time employees should repeat what they wrote down to make sure that they have a clear understanding of what the leader explained to them. Many times this is where the coaching plan fails. Leaders have many years of experience and job knowledge that the employee does not have initially, and many times they explain things above the employee's knowledge level. Writing down and repeating responses is a good method to ensure clarity and understanding.

STEP 6 Continue with constant feedback on performance and continue to monitor; if deficiencies continue, repeat step 5.

STEP 7 Employee performance should be corrected by this point. If it is not, then it is possible that this employee is in the wrong job. This person does not have the required skill set or aptitude to do the job properly. At this time a few things can be done. If the employees in question are in good standing, you can look to transfer them to another position that they are qualified for and will be successful at. If they are not in good standing, you may not have any other option but to end their employment with your company.

Montanez emphasizes improved employee performance surrounded by quality coaching and training. These are the tools for success. Montanez adds, "You must provide ongoing training for continued success in the workplace so that your employees know that you value them and are willing to train them in other areas, once they are competent in their current position.

"Employee coaching and development plans were created to assist an employee in getting back on track to positive work performance. Our philosophy is to give employees the coaching and development that they need to become successful within our organization," says Montanez.

"Our development of the employee always begins with training and at least 60 days of constant feedback on performance for all new duties assigned. This gives the employee a chance to develop at their own pace and ask questions to help them in their understanding. Once the 60 days of training is complete, then the employees are held to normal performance standards for quality and productivity. If the employee fails in quality or productivity, they are placed on a formal Employee Coaching and Development Plan. This plan provides information on their deficiency and an action plan for improvement.

"During the formal Coaching and Development Plan, the employee receives more training and constant feedback, both positive and negative. We believe in a "Praise in Progress" methodology and a "Direct and Specific Feedback" methodology. This way we assist our employees every step of the way," adds Montanez.

"Our employees receive four chances within a one-year timeline to improve their performance. If improvement is not noted, then unfortunately separation of employment may occur. If they are unable to improve, we may look to other departments that have openings to evaluate if their skills are transferrable to the other department. We will only do a transfer, if the employee is in good standing with attendance and their record must be clear from policy violations. Our reasoning behind this is we do not want to transfer a problem employee to another manager or supervisor.

"Below you will find some of our most used templates for employee improvement, with a wide range of deficiencies detailed. The templates are used to target productivity, quality, attendance, and policy violations. These templates can be modified to meet your immediate needs to improve employee performance.

"The most valuable tool that a company can have is its ability to document conversations, track performance, both positive and negative, and maintain positive relations with its employees. The most successful companies play to their employees' strengths and help them to excel to greatness by doing this," says Montanez.

Seven Steps to Handling Employee Performance Problems

Visit www.HumanResourcesSources.org and download this MP3 audio interview to get the latest advice on improving employee performance in a changing workplace, along with ongoing tips, tools, and techniques for HR professionals and other leaders.

Listen to and learn from the interview with HR subject-matter expert and popular human resources thought leader, Stephanie Montanez, on her Problem Solving Tool Kit for Employee Performance Improvement, which contains seven steps to success.

Highlights of the MP3 interview include:

1. How-tos for supporting employees and improving on-the-job performance issues, such as attendance, job performance, and more.
2. Considering alternate positions for employees when job performance is under par.
3. Correcting job deficiencies with an overall set program and plan to follow.
4. Offering HR professionals proactive advice for their employee performance challenges.
5. How to prepare yourself for difficult conversations.
6. How to work with your employees to increase learning on the job.
7. How to kick up your coaching style.

HumanResourcesSources.org is an invaluable resource for HR professionals and leaders, and the go-to source for HR downloads and links to the latest tips on improving employee and workplace performance problems, employee development coaching and training, as well as ongoing assistance with talent branding.

Following are 14 Employee Coaching and Development Plan templates that Stephanie has found effective and recommends trying.

EMPLOYEE COACHING AND DEVELOPMENT PLAN			
Employee:	Alice Cummings		
Position:		Department/Team:	
Date of Hire:		Date of Conference:	
Type of Performance Management			
☐ Verbal Warning	☐ First Written Warning	☐ Second Written Warning	☒ Final Written Warning
Termination:			
Other Action (specify):			

Reason for Performance Management

☒ Unsatisfactory performance or conduct
☐ Other (specify):

Description: *Provide a short, factual explanation of the reason for performance management. Please indicate if there have been previous counseling sessions.*

As outlined in the Company Employee Handbook it is expected that all employees will conduct themselves with the pride and respect associated with their positions, fellow employees, clients, and the Company business. Any employee demonstrating improper conduct will be subject to disciplinary action up to and including termination of employment.

On Friday, [Date], Alice was given work to complete by the end of the same business day, since all accounts were noted with the [Date] date as being mailed. The next business day it was discovered that Alice took the work that she was given on Friday, [Date], and placed it on a coworker's desk without completing it. This was in direct opposition to the instructions she was given by her manager, Michelle Smart.

This incident constitutes violations of the General Rules of Conduct Policy, in the sections below:

- Incompletion of the assigned work resulted in restricting output of work and an interruption of department production and accounts being updated with the incorrect date.
- Gross insubordination—a willful and deliberate refusal to follow reasonable orders given by a member of management, by failing to perform the job functions that were assigned to her.
- Performing a substandard quantity of work by not completing tasks assigned to her by a manager.

As a result of her actions, Alice is being issued a final written warning. She had previous warnings for similar behavior on [Date] and [Date].

Action Plan for Improvement: *Identify specific solutions, expectations, and time frame for improvement. Use additional sheets as necessary.*

- Alice must follow instructions given for completing work at all times and must not modify her work or the work of others without direction from management.
- If Alice is unclear about how to perform the work given, she must notify her manager or assigned supervisor.
- Any acts of retaliation to coworkers will not be tolerated and will result in immediate termination of employment.
- Future incidents of insubordination may result in further disciplinary action up to and including immediate termination.

Failure to improve to the expected performance standard while on a written performance improvement plan may result in termination of employment.

While the plan may indicate a specific duration, it is not an employment contract for the specified time period.

Following successful completion of the plan, documentation acknowledging your performance improvement will be placed in your personnel file. **Should unsatisfactory performance recur within the next 12 months, further action will be taken up to and including termination of employment.**

Please recognize the seriousness of this message and feel free to discuss questions or concerns with your Supervisor, Manager, or the Director of Human Resource while we work together to get your performance back on track.

Employee Comments: *(use additional sheets as necessary)*

Your signature is intended only to acknowledge receipt of the notice; it does not imply agreement or disagreement. Your signature implies understanding that this document will be placed in your personnel file.

Employee:	Date:
Immediate Supervisor:	Date:
Department Manager:	Date:
Human Resources:	Date:
☐ A copy of this document has been provided to the employee.	
Date:	Supervisor Initials:

EMPLOYEE COACHING AND DEVELOPMENT PLAN

Employee:	Norman Bussing	
Position:		Department/Team:
Date of Hire:		Date of Conference:

Type of Performance Management

☒ Verbal Warning	☐ First Written Warning	☐ Second Written Warning	☐ Final Written Warning

Termination:

Other Action (specify):

Reason for Performance Management

☒ Unsatisfactory performance or conduct
☐ Other (specify):

Description: *Provide a short, factual explanation of the reason for performance management. Please indicate if there have been previous counseling sessions.*

It is the responsibility of an Assistant Supervisor to meet these essential qualifications (taken from the position description:

- Assists in the training and auditing of new employees
- Assists in the planning, assigning, and directing of work
- Assists in addressing internal/external complaints
- Excellent verbal communication skills
- Strong interpersonal skills to work within a team environment
- Demonstrate effective customer service skills with internal and external customers
- Ability to present information in one-on-one and small group situations

In order to coach Norman to meet each of the above listed qualifications, formal feedback forms along with documented counseling sessions have been provided.

- February Feedback form
- March Feedback form
- August Feedback form
- September Feedback form
- Annual Performance Evaluations
- October Verbal Warning for managing Los Gatos Work in Progress
- December Feedback form
- Various counseling sessions with Supervisor: [Date] and [Date]
- Q1 Feedback form
- Q2 Feedback form
- [Date], counseling session with Supervisor and Regional Manager

After two years in the position, progress is expected to be evident. At this point, his performance is still considered not meeting standards. Also, progress with leadership qualities is not being made, including the items listed below:

- Inaccurate auditing and account review
- Lack of interest in creating new processes or refining old ones

- Dealing with employee discipline issues
- Taking ownership of projects assigned
- Follow-up with employees if he has delegated work
- Poor listening skills
- Identifying areas of self-development
- Taking advantage of leadership training opportunities
- Setting an example of being a leader to all other employees

Action Plan for Improvement: *Identify specific solutions, expectations, and time frame for improvement. Use additional sheets as necessary.*

- Develop a personal performance plan on how to improve in the areas listed above. This written development plan will be due one week from the date of conference referenced on this action plan and a copy will be maintained with this document.
- Foster and maintain positive client (internal and external) relations
- Exhibit strong leadership skills
- Display excellent verbal communication skills as well as strong interpersonal skills
- Further incidents of this nature may result in additional corrective action up to and including termination of employment.

Failure to improve to the expected performance standard while on a written performance improvement plan may result in termination of employment.

While the plan may indicate a specific duration, it is not an employment contract for the specified time period.

Following successful completion of the plan, documentation acknowledging your performance improvement will be placed in your personnel file. **Should unsatisfactory performance recur within the next 12 months, further action will be taken up to and including termination of employment.**

Please recognize the seriousness of this message and feel free to discuss questions or concerns with your Supervisor, Manager, or the Director of Human Resource while we work together to get your performance back on track.

Employee Comments: *(use additional sheets as necessary)*

Your signature is intended only to acknowledge receipt of the notice; it does not imply agreement or disagreement. Your signature implies understanding that this document will be placed in your personnel file.

Employee:	Date:
Immediate Supervisor:	Date:
Department Manager:	Date:
Human Resources:	Date:
☐ A copy of this document has been provided to the employee.	
Date:	Supervisor Initials:

EMPLOYEE COACHING AND DEVELOPMENT PLAN

Employee:	Doris Swensen	
Position:		Department/Team:
Date of Hire:		Date of Conference:

Type of Performance Management

☒ Verbal Warning	☐ First Written Warning	☐ Second Written Warning	☐ Final Written Warning

Termination:

Other Action (specify):

Reason for Performance Management

☒ Unsatisfactory performance or conduct
☐ Other (specify):

Description: *Provide a short, factual explanation of the reason for performance management. Please indicate if there have been previous counseling sessions.*

The Company handbook states, under the General Rules of Conduct, "The Company expects that all of its employees will conduct themselves with appropriate pride and respect associated with their positions, fellow employees, clients, and the Company. Employees should always use good judgment and discretion in carrying out the Company's business. The highest standards of ethical conduct should always be used by employees of the Company. Improper conduct by and between employees and/or by and between employees and business associates on the Company's premises that adversely affects Company work will not be tolerated. Any employee demonstrating improper conduct will be subject to disciplinary action up to and including termination of employment.

Some examples of misconduct for which discipline will be warranted include:
- Gross insubordination—a willful and deliberate refusal to follow reasonable orders given by a member of management.
- Restricting output, or persuading others to do so, or promoting, encouraging, agitating, engaging in, or supporting suspension of work, slowdowns, or any other interruptions of production.

On [Date], Doris attended a team meeting in which her Supervisor, Henry Gold, instructed all members of the team that they were to put all other work aside and post charts until they were all done. This was an instruction given by the Manager so that the team could reach its month-end charge goal. During the day, Henry Gold checked in with Doris, and found that she had not posted any charts and was working on her write off report. Henry Gold instructed her to put her report away and start posting charts. At the end of the day Doris posted 21 charts.

Also during the meeting that Doris attended on [Date], her Assistant Supervisor announced that she would be leaving the company in the spring. Doris made the comment that no one on the team could apply for her position anyway because the company will not take anyone out of the team.

Doris was instructed to complete all assigned payment batches by the end of the day on [Date]. At the end of the day she had 5 batches that were still not posted. She did not communicate to her Supervisor or Assistant Supervisor that she was not able to finish them so no one was able to assist with meeting this deadline.

On [Date], Doris slammed down her phone and yelled "Come on already." Her Assistant Supervisor got up to see what was going on. Doris was working on her write off report and had become frustrated.

It is required that employees conduct themselves in a manner that is respectful to others, in accordance with the General Rules of Conduct. Our purpose at the Company is to provide excellent service to our clients. This service includes billing out their claims and posting their payments in a timely manner. In order to achieve this, monthly targets have been set and all team members must work under the direction of their management team to achieve these targets.

Action Plan for Improvement: *Identify specific solutions, expectations, and time frame for improvement. Use additional sheets as necessary.*

- Doris must post all payment batches assigned to her within 48 hours.
- At the end of the month, Doris will post all batches assigned to her prior to the cutoff date.
- If Doris is unable to meet an assigned deadline, she will communicate this to her Supervisor immediately so that the work may be delegated to meet the deadline.
- Doris will refrain from making derogatory statements that negatively impact the morale of the team.
- Further incidents of this nature will be cause for additional disciplinary action up to and including termination of employment.

Failure to improve to the expected performance standard while on a written performance improvement plan may result in termination of employment.

While the plan may indicate a specific duration, it is not an employment contract for the specified time period.

Following successful completion of the plan, documentation acknowledging your performance improvement will be placed in your personnel file. **Should unsatisfactory performance recur within the next 12 months, further action will be taken up to and including termination of employment.**

Please recognize the seriousness of this message and feel free to discuss questions or concerns with your Supervisor, Manager, or the Director of Human Resource while we work together to get your performance back on track.

Employee Comments: *(use additional sheets as necessary)*

Your signature is intended only to acknowledge receipt of the notice; it does not imply agreement or disagreement. Your signature implies understanding that this document will be placed in your personnel file.

Employee:	Date:
Immediate Supervisor:	Date:
Department Manager:	Date:
Human Resources:	Date:
☐ A copy of this document has been provided to the employee.	
Date:	Supervisor Initials:

EMPLOYEE COACHING AND DEVELOPMENT PLAN

Employee:	Brenda Santos	
Position:		Department/Team:
Date of Hire:		Date of Conference:

Type of Performance Management

☐ Verbal Warning	☒ First Written Warning	☐ Second Written Warning	☐ Final Written Warning

Termination:

Other (specify):

Reason for Performance Management

☐ Unsatisfactory performance or conduct
☒ Other (specify): Violation of No Harassment Policy and General Rules of Conduct

Description: *Provide a short, factual explanation of the reason for performance management. Please indicate if there have been previous counseling sessions.*

The Company does not tolerate any unwanted or unwelcome comments by or between coworkers. The company has zero tolerance for any type of disrespectful behavior and is committed to a workplace free of unprofessional behavior. Per the expectations set forth in our General Rules of Conduct, any employee demonstrating improper conduct will be subject to disciplinary action up to and including termination of employment.

- Brenda failed to follow the No Harassment Policy and General Rules of Conduct on [Date].
- Brenda engaged in a string of text messages with Monica throughout working hours on [Date].
- The content of the text messages was deemed inappropriate and violated the No Harassment Policy.
- The No Harassment Policy indicates, "Sexual advances, flirtations, obscene or vulgar gestures, posters or comments"; "conduct or comments consistently targeted at only one gender."

Action Plan for Improvement: *Identify specific solutions, expectations, and time frame for improvement. Use additional sheets as necessary.*

- Brenda must follow all of the policies and procedures set forth by the Company.
- Failure to follow the policies and procedures may result in additional corrective action up to and including termination of employment.
- Any additional messages or substantiated complaints of this nature will result in immediate termination of employment.
- The company has a No-Retaliation Policy. If substantiated retaliation occurs, Brenda will be subject to immediate termination.

Failure to improve to the expected performance standard while on a written performance improvement plan may result in termination of employment.

While the plan may indicate a specific duration, it is not an employment contract for the specified time period.

Following successful completion of the plan, documentation acknowledging your performance improvement will be placed in your personnel file. **Should unsatisfactory performance recur within the next 12 months, further action will be taken up to and including termination of employment.**

Please recognize the seriousness of this message and feel free to discuss questions or concerns with your Supervisor, Manager, or the Director of Human Resource while we work together to get your performance back on track.

Employee Comments: *(use additional sheets as necessary)*

Your signature is intended only to acknowledge receipt of the notice; it does not imply agreement or disagreement. Your signature implies understanding that this document will be placed in your personnel file.

Employee:	Date:
Immediate Supervisor:	Date:
Department Manager:	Date:
Human Resources:	Date:
☐ A copy of this document has been provided to the employee.	
Date:	Supervisor Initials:

EMPLOYEE COACHING AND DEVELOPMENT PLAN

Employee:	Lily Steinbeck	
Position:		Department/Team:
Date of Hire:		Date of Conference:

Type of Performance Management

☒ Verbal Warning	☐ First Written Warning	☐ Second Written Warning	☐ Final Written Warning

Termination:

Other Action (specify):

Reason for Performance Management

☐ Unsatisfactory performance or conduct
☒ Other (specify): 1. Violation of General Rules of Conduct 2. Violation of Cell Phone Policy

Description: *Provide a short, factual explanation of the reason for performance management. Please indicate if there have been previous counseling sessions.*

Per the expectations set forth in our General Rules of Conduct, any employee demonstrating improper conduct will be subject to disciplinary action up to and including termination of employment.

The Company's continued success depends on each and every employee's focused effort. While at work, efforts should be dedicated solely to the efficient completion of work-related tasks. During business hours, personal cell phones must be turned off and placed in a secure place (not on the workstation or in your pocket). You may use the device during your rest and meal period in the break room or outside the building.

- On [Date], Lily engaged in a string of text messages with Rhonda Stone during work hours. Text messaging during work hours is in violation of the Cell Phone Policy.
- Text messaging during work hours constitutes a violation of the General Rules of Conduct for restricting the output of production and persuading others to do so, promoting, encouraging, and suspending work.

Action Plan for Improvement: *Identify specific solutions, expectations, and time frame for improvement. Use additional sheets as necessary.*

- Lily must cease from sending text messages during work hours. In compliance with the Cell Phone Policy, Lily must keep her cell phone turned off and put away during her scheduled shift.
- Further violations of company policy will result in additional disciplinary action up to and including termination of employment.

Failure to improve to the expected performance standard while on a written performance improvement plan may result in termination of employment.

While the plan may indicate a specific duration, it is not an employment contract for the specified time period.

Following successful completion of the plan, documentation acknowledging your performance improvement will be placed in your personnel file. **Should unsatisfactory performance recur within the next 12 months, further action will be taken up to and including termination of employment.**

Please recognize the seriousness of this message and feel free to discuss questions or concerns with your Supervisor, Manager, or the Director of Human Resource while we work together to get your performance back on track.

Employee Comments: *(use additional sheets as necessary)*

Your signature is intended only to acknowledge receipt of the notice; it does not imply agreement or disagreement. Your signature implies understanding that this document will be placed in your personnel file.	
Employee:	Date:
Immediate Supervisor:	Date:
Department Manager:	Date:
Human Resources:	Date:
☐ A copy of this document has been provided to the employee.	
Date:	Supervisor Initials:

EMPLOYEE COACHING AND DEVELOPMENT PLAN

Employee:	Mark Ellison		
Position:		Department/Team:	
Date of Hire:		Date of Conference:	

Type of Performance Management

☐ Verbal Warning	☒ First Written Warning	☐ Second Written Warning	☐ Final Written Warning

Termination:

Other Action (specify):

Reason for Performance Management

☐ Unsatisfactory performance or conduct
☒ Other (specify): 1. Violation of General Rules of Conduct 2. Violation of Cell Phone Policy

Description: *Provide a short, factual explanation of the reason for performance management. Please indicate if there have been previous counseling sessions.*

The company has zero tolerance for any type of disrespectful behavior and is committed to a workplace free of unprofessional behavior. Per the expectations set forth in our General Rules of Conduct, any employee demonstrating improper conduct will be subject to disciplinary action up to and including termination of employment.

The Company's continued success depends on each and every employee's focused effort. While at work, efforts should be dedicated solely to the efficient completion of work-related tasks. During business hours, personal cell phones must be turned off and placed in a secure place (not on the workstation or in your pocket). You may use the device during your rest and meal period in the break room or outside the building.

- On [Date], Mark engaged in a string of text messages with Michael Stevens during work hours. Text messaging during work hours is in violation of the Cell Phone Policy.
- Text messaging during work hours constitutes a violation of the General Rules of Conduct for restricting the output of production and persuading others to do so, promoting, encouraging, and suspending work.
- Mark was observed on several occasions lying back relaxing and/or dozing in his chair.
- Mark was observed throwing notes to two other coders. This behavior is unproductive not only for Mark, but is also distracting and disruptive to his coworkers and their productivity.

Mark previously received a Verbal Warning on [Date] regarding violations of the General Rules of Conduct, for excessive socializing, taking unscheduled breaks, and leaving the premises during break.

These additional violations prompt a First Written Warning.

Action Plan for Improvement: *Identify specific solutions, expectations, and time frame for improvement. Use additional sheets as necessary.*

- Mark must cease from sending text messages during work hours. In compliance with the Cell Phone Policy, Mark must keep his cell phone turned off and put away during his scheduled shift.
- Mark must cease from disruptive behavior in the work area.
- Further violations of company policy will result in additional disciplinary action up to and including termination of employment.

Failure to improve to the expected performance standard while on a written performance improvement plan may result in termination of employment.

While the plan may indicate a specific duration, it is not an employment contract for the specified time period.

Following successful completion of the plan, documentation acknowledging your performance improvement will be placed in your personnel file. **Should unsatisfactory performance recur within the next 12 months, further action will be taken up to and including termination of employment.**

Please recognize the seriousness of this message and feel free to discuss questions or concerns with your Supervisor, Manager, or the Director of Human Resource while we work together to get your performance back on track.

Employee Comments: *(use additional sheets as necessary)*

Your signature is intended only to acknowledge receipt of the notice; it does not imply agreement or disagreement. Your signature implies understanding that this document will be placed in your personnel file.

Employee:	Date:
Immediate Supervisor:	Date:
Department Manager:	Date:
Human Resources:	Date:
☐ A copy of this document has been provided to the employee.	
Date:	Supervisor Initials:

EMPLOYEE COACHING AND DEVELOPMENT PLAN

Employee:	Jermaine Johnson	
Position:		Department/Team:
Date of Hire:		Date of Conference:

Type of Performance Management

☐ Verbal Warning	☒ First Written Warning	☐ Second Written Warning	☐ Final Written Warning

Termination:

Other Action (specify):

Reason for Performance Management

☐ Unsatisfactory performance or conduct
☒ Other (specify): Violation of Harassment Policy and General Rules of Conduct

Description: *Provide a short, factual explanation of the reason for performance management. Please indicate if there have been previous counseling sessions.*

The Company does not tolerate any unwanted or unwelcome comments by or between coworkers. The company has zero tolerance for any type of disrespectful behavior and is committed to a workplace free of unprofessional behavior. Per the expectations set forth in our General Rules of Conduct, any employee demonstrating improper conduct will be subject to disciplinary action up to and including termination of employment.

* Jermaine failed to follow the No Harassment Policy and General Rules of Conduct on [Date].
* Jermaine engaged in a string of text messages with Marvin Lewis throughout working hours [Date].
* The content of the text messages was deemed inappropriate and violated the No Harassment Policy.

The No Harassment Policy indicates, "Sexual advances, flirtations, obscene or vulgar gestures, posters or comments"; "conduct or comments consistently targeted at only one gender."

Action Plan for Improvement: *Identify specific solutions, expectations, and time frame for improvement. Use additional sheets as necessary.*

- Jermaine must follow all of the policies and procedures set forth by the Company.
- Failure to follow the policies and procedures may result in additional corrective action up to and including termination of employment.
- Any additional messages or substantiated complaints of this nature will result in immediate termination of employment.
- The company has a No-Retaliation Policy. If substantiated retaliation occurs, Jermaine will be subject to immediate termination.

Failure to improve to the expected performance standard while on a written performance improvement plan may result in termination of employment.

While the plan may indicate a specific duration, it is not an employment contract for the specified time period.

Following successful completion of the plan, documentation acknowledging your performance improvement will be placed in your personnel file. **Should unsatisfactory performance recur within the next 12 months, further action will be taken up to and including termination of employment.**

Please recognize the seriousness of this message and feel free to discuss questions or concerns with your Supervisor, Manager, or the Director of Human Resource while we work together to get your performance back on track.

Employee Comments: *(use additional sheets as necessary)*

Your signature is intended only to acknowledge receipt of the notice; it does not imply agreement or disagreement. Your signature implies understanding that this document will be placed in your personnel file.	
Employee:	Date:
Immediate Supervisor:	Date:
Department Manager:	Date:
Human Resources:	Date:
☐ A copy of this document has been provided to the employee.	
Date:	Supervisor Initials:

EMPLOYEE COACHING AND DEVELOPMENT PLAN

Employee:	Veronica Rodriguez	
Position:		Department/Team:
Date of Hire:		Date of Conference:

Type of Performance Management

☒ Verbal Warning	☐ First Written Warning	☐ Second Written Warning	☐ Final Written Warning

Termination:

Other Action (specify):

Reason for Performance Management

☐ Unsatisfactory performance or conduct
☒ Other (specify): Violation of Personal Cell Phone Policy

Description: *Provide a short, factual explanation of the reason for performance management. Please indicate if there have been previous counseling sessions.*

As stated in the "Cell Phones, Pagers, PDAs" policy in the Employee Handbook: During business hours, these devices MUST be turned off and placed in a secure place (i.e., your purse or desk drawer), not on the workstation or in your pocket. You may use the devices during your rest and meal periods in the break room or outside the building."

- [Date]—Veronica's supervisor held a team meeting and stressed that cell phones must be turned OFF while employees are on the workroom floor.
- [Date]—Team meeting: reminder that phone must be turned off.
- [Date]—Veronica's supervisor received a complaint that Veronica was text messaging on her cell phone in the middle of an accelerated training class. (When questioned, Veronica denied having her phone with her in the room.) Veronica was asked to review the cell phone policy and sign an acknowledgment signifying her understanding of the policy.
- [Date]—Team meeting: reminder that phone must be in OFF position.
- [Date]—Veronica's supervisor approached Veronica in her cubicle and found her phone in her hand at her workstation. The phone was in the "ON" position.

Veronica has been instructed on multiple occasions regarding the use of cell phones; therefore, Veronica is being presented with a documented Verbal Warning at this time.

Action Plan for Improvement: *Identify specific solutions, expectations, and time frame for improvement. Use additional sheets as necessary.*

- Veronica must immediately and consistently comply with company policy in regard to cell phones. Her phone must be kept in a secure place during work hours and kept in the OFF position until she is in the break room or outside—during her assigned break time or lunch period.
- Any further violations of this policy will result in further disciplinary action.
- Veronica is being asked to read the Cell Phone Policy and sign another acknowledgment form to signify her understanding of the policy.

Failure to improve to the expected performance standard while on a written performance improvement plan may result in termination of employment.

While the plan may indicate a specific duration, it is not an employment contract for the specified time period.

Following successful completion of the plan, documentation acknowledging your performance improvement will be placed in your personnel file. **Should unsatisfactory performance recur within the next 12 months, further action will be taken up to and including termination of employment.**

Please recognize the seriousness of this message and feel free to discuss questions or concerns with your Supervisor, Manager, or the Director of Human Resource while we work together to get your performance back on track.

Employee Comments: *(use additional sheets as necessary)*

Your signature is intended only to acknowledge receipt of the notice; it does not imply agreement or disagreement. Your signature implies understanding that this document will be placed in your personnel file.

Employee:	Date:
Immediate Supervisor:	Date:
Department Manager:	Date:
Human Resources:	Date:
☐ A copy of this document has been provided to the employee.	
Date:	Supervisor Initials:

EMPLOYEE COACHING AND DEVELOPMENT PLAN

Employee:	Sally Browning	
Position:		Department/Team:
Date of Hire:		Date of Conference:

Type of Performance Management

☒ Verbal Warning	☐ First Written Warning	☐ Second Written Warning	☐ Final Written Warning

Termination:

Other Action (specify):

Reason for Performance Management

☐ Unsatisfactory performance or conduct
☒ Other (specify): Company Safety Policy Violation

Description: *Provide a short, factual explanation of the reason for performance management. Please indicate if there have been previous counseling sessions.*

Sally has not been in compliance with the Company's Safety Policy.

A complaint was received on [Date] in which Sally was witnessed driving at an unsafe speed in the Company parking lot, which is in violation of the Company's Safety Policy. Sally was previously witnessed driving at an unsafe speed and therefore is being given this written verbal warning.

The Company is committed to providing a safe and healthy workplace for all its employees. It is the policy of the Company to protect the safety and health of our employees to the best of our ability, and therefore the Company requires that employees drive no more than five (5) miles per hour in the parking lots.

Action Plan for Improvement: *Identify specific solutions, expectations, and time frame for improvement. Use additional sheets as necessary.*

- Sally must adhere to all the Company's Safety Policies including, but not limited to, driving no more than five (5) miles per hour in the parking lots.
- Further incidents of policy violations may result in further disciplinary action up to and including immediate termination of employment.

Failure to improve to the expected performance standard while on a written performance improvement plan may result in termination of employment.

While the plan may indicate a specific duration, it is not an employment contract for the specified time period.

Following successful completion of the plan, documentation acknowledging your performance improvement will be placed in your personnel file. **Should unsatisfactory performance recur within the next 12 months, further action will be taken up to and including termination of employment.**

Please recognize the seriousness of this message and feel free to discuss questions or concerns with your Supervisor, Manager, or the Director of Human Resource while we work together to get your performance back on track.

Employee Comments: *(use additional sheets as necessary)*

Your signature is intended only to acknowledge receipt of the notice; it does not imply agreement or disagreement. Your signature implies understanding that this document will be placed in your personnel file.

Employee:	Date:
Immediate Supervisor:	Date:
Department Manager:	Date:
Human Resources:	Date:
☐ A copy of this document has been provided to the employee.	
Date:	Supervisor Initials:

EMPLOYEE COACHING AND DEVELOPMENT PLAN

Employee:	Roderick Dickens	
Position:		Department/Team:
Date of Hire:		Date of Conference:

Type of Performance Management

☐ Verbal Warning	☒ First Written Warning	☐ Second Written Warning	☐ Final Written Warning

Termination:

Other Action (specify):

Reason for Performance Management

☐ Unsatisfactory performance or conduct
☒ Other (specify): Violation against the timekeeping system and usage of cell phone during working hours

Description: *Provide a short, factual explanation of the reason for performance management. Please indicate if there have been previous counseling sessions.*

On [Date], while I was at lunch, I observed Roderick driving into the Company parking lot at approximately 11:25 a.m. talking on his cell phone. He parked his car while on his cell phone, stood outside, and continued to talk. At 11:32 a.m. he went into the building to punch in and came back outside and continued talking on his cell phone. He went back into the building at approximately 11:36 a.m.

Roderick violated our Attendance Record policy which states the following: "Please be ready to work and proceed directly to your workstation after punching in."

In addition, Roderick violated the company cell phone policy which states the following: "You are requested to refrain from using personal cell phones, pagers, or other similar devices to conduct personal business while at work."

My department has held two meetings this year pertaining to cell phone usage during company time. Roderick was present during both meetings. He signed the meeting agendas on [Date] and [Date]. At this time Roderick will receive a First Written Warning for violation of the timekeeping system and cell phone usage.

This incident constitutes violations of the General Rules of Conduct Policy, the timekeeping policy, and the personal cell phone policy in the sections below:

- Falsification of production records by not working when on the clock, causing his production to be inaccurate.
- Falsification of time records for taking an unauthorized break during a nonbreak time.
- Restricting output of work and interrupting production.
- Gross insubordination—a willful and deliberate refusal to follow reasonable orders given by a member of management, by failing to perform the job functions that were assigned to him.
- Performing a substandard quantity of work by using the telephone for personal use during work time.
- Violating the Use of Company Telephones, Personal Cell Phones, Pagers, and Other Similar Devices at Work Policy by making personal phone calls while on company paid time.

Action Plan for Improvement: *Identify specific solutions, expectations, and time frame for improvement. Use additional sheets as necessary.*

- Roderick shall refrain from using the telephone for personal use when he is supposed to be performing work duties.
- Roderick must work as instructed to do so and follow all company policies and adhere to the general rules of conduct at all times.
- Failure to improve to the expected performance standard while on a written performance improvement plan may result in additional corrective action up to and including immediate termination of employment.

Failure to improve to the expected performance standard while on a written performance improvement plan may result in termination of employment.

While the plan may indicate a specific duration, it is not an employment contract for the specified time period.

Following successful completion of the plan, documentation acknowledging your performance improvement will be placed in your personnel file. **Should unsatisfactory performance recur within the next 12 months, further action will be taken up to and including termination of employment.**

Please recognize the seriousness of this message and feel free to discuss questions or concerns with your Supervisor, Manager, or the Director of Human Resource while we work together to get your performance back on track.

Employee Comments: *(use additional sheets as necessary)*

Your signature is intended only to acknowledge receipt of the notice; it does not imply agreement or disagreement. Your signature implies understanding that this document will be placed in your personnel file.

Employee:	Date:
Immediate Supervisor:	Date:
Department Manager:	Date:
Human Resources:	Date:
☐ A copy of this document has been provided to the employee.	
Date:	Supervisor Initials:

EMPLOYEE COACHING AND DEVELOPMENT PLAN

Employee:	Mary Cleage	
Position:		Department/Team:
Date of Hire:		Date of Conference:

Type of Performance Management

☒ Verbal Warning	☐ First Written Warning	☐ Second Written Warning	☐ Final Written Warning

Termination:

Other Action (specify):

Reason for Performance Management

☐ Unsatisfactory performance or conduct
☒ Other (specify): Personal Phone Use—Social Networking Twitter Use

Description: *Provide a short, factual explanation of the reason for performance management. Please indicate if there have been previous counseling sessions.*

Mary has been given the Company Employee Handbook, specifically the section on Use of Company Telephones, Personal Cell Phones, Pagers, and Other Similar Devices at Work. Based on Twitter records, Mary has made excessive personal "tweets" and inappropriate comments with regard to confidential information and is in violation of the above policy.

Action Plan for Improvement: *Identify specific solutions, expectations, and time frame for improvement. Use additional sheets as necessary.*

- Adhere to the Company policy regarding Use of Company Telephones, Personal Cell Phones, Pagers, and Other Similar Devices at Work. Personal business must be handled outside of working hours.
- Refrain from discussing or writing about confidential information or sensitive material.
- If excessive personal cell phone or social networking continues, additional disciplinary action may be taken up to and including immediate termination of employment.

Failure to improve to the expected performance standard while on a written performance improvement plan may result in termination of employment.

While the plan may indicate a specific duration, it is not an employment contract for the specified time period.

Following successful completion of the plan, documentation acknowledging your performance improvement will be placed in your personnel file. **Should unsatisfactory performance recur within the next 12 months, further action will be taken up to and including termination of employment.**

Please recognize the seriousness of this message and feel free to discuss questions or concerns with your Supervisor, Manager, or the Director of Human Resource while we work together to get your performance back on track.

Employee Comments: *(use additional sheets as necessary)*

Your signature is intended only to acknowledge receipt of the notice; it does not imply agreement or disagreement. Your signature implies understanding that this document will be placed in your personnel file.

Employee:	Date:
Immediate Supervisor:	Date:
Department Manager:	Date:
Human Resources:	Date:
☐ A copy of this document has been provided to the employee.	
Date:	Supervisor Initials:

EMPLOYEE COACHING AND DEVELOPMENT PLAN		
Employee:	Michelle Jennings	
Position:		Department/Team:
Date of Hire:		Date of Conference:

Type of Performance Management

☐ Verbal Warning	☒ First Written Warning	☐ Second Written Warning	☐ Final Written Warning

Termination:

Other Action (specify):

Reason for Performance Management

☒ Unsatisfactory performance or conduct
   For failing to abide by Timekeeping Policy / Falsifying Time for Break Period
☐ Other (specify):

Description: *Provide a short, factual explanation of the reason for performance management. Please indicate if there have been previous counseling sessions.*

On [Date] at [Time], Kaye Whiteside witnessed Michelle entering the bottom left-hand drawer of the desk of Jane Rossi who was out of the office for the day. When Kaye Whiteside noticed Michelle reaching in the desk, Michelle immediately departed the cubicle and left the building through the main entrance. Kaye Whiteside reported it to her manager, and at that time an investigation began. Here's what the investigation revealed:

- Michelle departed for her afternoon break period at [Time] and returned from her break at [Time], failing to return from her break within 15 minutes.
- Michelle is scheduled for her daily break period from [Break Time]. On [Date], Michelle failed to follow her scheduled break period. Kaye Whiteside notified her Regional Manager at [Time] of Michelle's late departure on that day, and also the strange behavior of gaining access to another employee's desk.
- The team's break time record was reviewed by Kaye Whiteside, and the Regional Manager, which confirmed that Michelle failed to enter her break period prior to her departure.
- Upon Michelle's return to the office, she entered both "IN" and "OUT" break times as OUT: [Time] and IN: [Time]. This would have indicated a _____-minute break period when in truth Michelle had begun her break at [Time] and returned at [Time], which gave her a _____-minute break.
- Kaye Whiteside also talked with Michelle regarding why she had entered the desk of the absent employee. Michelle responded, "I was getting some Ibuprofen from the first aid bag within her desk." We counseled Michelle never to enter an employee's desk, unless she was given explicit permission to do so.

Action Plan for Improvement: *Identify specific solutions, expectations, and time frame for improvement. Use additional sheets as necessary.*

- Michelle will need to abide by the team break period schedule.
- Michelle must obtain approval to enter anyone's desk or to take items from a desk. Failure to obtain approval may result in disciplinary action, up to and including termination of employment.
- Further instances of falsifying break schedule or timekeeping may result in additional disciplinary action up to and including termination of employment.

Failure to improve to the expected performance standard while on a written performance improvement plan may result in termination of employment.

While the plan may indicate a specific duration, it is not an employment contract for the specified time period.

Following successful completion of the plan, documentation acknowledging your performance improvement will be placed in your personnel file. **Should unsatisfactory performance recur within the next 12 months, further action will be taken up to and including termination of employment.**

Please recognize the seriousness of this message and feel free to discuss questions or concerns with your Supervisor, Manager, or the Director of Human Resource while we work together to get your performance back on track.

Employee Comments: *(use additional sheets as necessary)*

Your signature is intended only to acknowledge receipt of the notice; it does not imply agreement or disagreement. Your signature implies understanding that this document will be placed in your personnel file.

Employee:	Date:
Immediate Supervisor:	Date:
Department Manager:	Date:
Human Resources:	Date:
☐ A copy of this document has been provided to the employee.	
Date:	Supervisor Initials:

EMPLOYEE COACHING AND DEVELOPMENT PLAN

Employee:	Frida Pearla	
Position:		Department/Team:
Date of Hire:		Date of Conference:

Type of Performance Management

☐ Verbal Warning	☒ First Written Warning	☐ Second Written Warning	☐ Final Written Warning

Termination:

Other Action (specify):

Reason for Performance Management

☒ Unsatisfactory performance or conduct
☐ Other (specify):

Description: *Provide a short, factual explanation of the reason for performance management. Please indicate if there have been previous counseling sessions.*

The Company's general rules of conduct require that all employees be respectful to fellow employees and clients. Improper conduct by and between employees and/or by and between employees and business associates on the Company's premises that adversely affects Company work will not be tolerated.

A conversation was held on [Date] with Frida and directive was given to her to cease solicitation and campaigning of employment for her son at the Company. On [Date], Frida approached her Regional Manager and apologized and stated, "I realize I have been too aggressive and should not have been involved in trying to have an employment offer be made to my son; I will drop it." The Regional Manager explained to her, "You need to allow the Company to perform fair hiring practices and hope for the best!" On [Date] during a Supervisor meeting, Frida's Supervisor alluded to a conversation held in the parking area on [Date] and again at her desk on [Date], saying that Frida again approached her about speaking to another supervisor about hiring her son.

I asked Frida and her Supervisor to come into my office. Frida understood the gravity of the situation because she seemed very nervous. I asked Frida, "I understand you had again approached your Supervisor after we spoke to you about not soliciting or campaigning employment for your son." I asked her why she had done this after we had specifically asked her to drop her pursuit and solicitation of employment for her son. At first, Frida denied this conversation happened and then eventually conceded and then responded, "Yes, I understood the conversation clearly but thought it was okay because Annabell Smith is a Supervisor." While this conversation was held during Frida's break period, I let her know that I was aware she was not on her break period at other times when she had approached the President and COO, Department Managers, Supervisors, and the HR Department regarding the status of her son's employment and hiring opportunity at the Company.

Action Plan for Improvement: *Identify specific solutions, expectations, and time frame for improvement. Use additional sheets as necessary.*

- Frida must follow all directives given to her from her Director, Regional Manager, and/or those in leadership positions. Failure to do so is considered insubordinate behavior which is a violation of the General Rules of Conduct policy, and will not be tolerated at the Company.
- Frida must refrain from soliciting or campaigning employment at the Company for friends or family members and allow them to go through the normal employment processes.
- Further incidents of this nature may result in further disciplinary action up to and including termination of employment.

Failure to improve to the expected performance standard while on a written performance improvement plan may result in termination of employment.

While the plan may indicate a specific duration, it is not an employment contract for the specified time period.

Following successful completion of the plan, documentation acknowledging your performance improvement will be placed in your personnel file. **Should unsatisfactory performance recur within the next 12 months, further action will be taken up to and including termination of employment.**

Please recognize the seriousness of this message and feel free to discuss questions or concerns with your Supervisor, Manager, or the Director of Human Resource while we work together to get your performance back on track.

Employee Comments: *(use additional sheets as necessary)*

Your signature is intended only to acknowledge receipt of the notice; it does not imply agreement or disagreement. Your signature implies understanding that this document will be placed in your personnel file.

Employee:	Date:
Immediate Supervisor:	Date:
Department Manager:	Date:
Human Resources:	Date:
□ A copy of this document has been provided to the employee.	
Date:	Supervisor Initials:

EMPLOYEE COACHING AND DEVELOPMENT PLAN	
Employee:	Sophia Lambretti
Position:	Department/Team:
Date of Hire:	Date of Conference:

Type of Performance Management			
☐ Verbal Warning	☐ First Written Warning	☐ Second Written Warning	☒ Final Written Warning

Termination:

Other Action (specify): Violating the Use of Company Telephones, Cell Phones, Pagers, and Other Similar Devices at Work, and the General Rules of Conduct policies.

Reason for Performance Management

☒ Unsatisfactory performance or conduct
☐ Other (specify):

Description: *Provide a short, factual explanation of the reason for performance management. Please indicate if there have been previous counseling sessions.*

On [Date], the payment department had its monthly training class. During the presentation, Sophia's Supervisor heard a cell phone vibrating. Sophia's Supervisor scanned the room to see if she could see whose phone it was. After the class, the Manager of the training department said to Sophia's Supervisor, "Do you know whose phone that was?" Sophia's Supervisor said "No." The Manager then told her it was Sophia's cell phone. She said when the phone started vibrating, Sophia put her hand over it and looked at her coworker next to her and said, "That's my phone. I forgot to turn it off."

On [Date], Sophia's Supervisor came into the break room and noticed Sophia in the break room talking on her cell phone. Sophia's Supervisor let her finish her conversation and approached her later asking if she was clocked in to work while she was on her phone. Sophia stated she had to take a call regarding her mother. She stated she had just got in the break room right before her Supervisor came in so she wasn't in there that long. Sophia's Supervisor told her that she can give her Supervisor's phone number to her family if needed, and her Supervisor will then transfer the calls to her. Her Supervisor told Sophia that she should not be on her cell phone at that time of morning, nor should her cell phone be on during work hours. Sophia understood.

This incident constitutes violations of the General Rules of Conduct Policy, in the sections below:
- Falsification of production records by not working when on the clock, causing her production to be inaccurate.
- Falsification of time records for taking an unauthorized break during a nonbreak time.
- Restricting output of work and interrupting production.
- Gross insubordination—a willful and deliberate refusal to follow reasonable orders given by a member of management, by failing to perform the job functions that were assigned to her.
- Performing a substandard quantity of work by using her personal cell phone during work time.
- Violating the Use of Company Telephones, Personal Cell Phones, Pagers, and Other Similar Devices at Work Policy by making excessive personal phone calls while on company paid time.

Action Plan for Improvement: *Identify specific solutions, expectations, and time frame for improvement. Use additional sheets as necessary.*

- Sophia shall refrain from using her cellular telephone for personal use when she is on the clock and should be engaged in work duties.
- Sophia must work as instructed and follow all company policies, adhering to the General Rules of Conduct at all times.
- Further incidents of this nature may result in further disciplinary action up to and including termination of employment.

Failure to improve to the expected performance standard while on a written performance improvement plan may result in termination of employment.

While the plan may indicate a specific duration, it is not an employment contract for the specified time period.

Following successful completion of the plan, documentation acknowledging your performance improvement will be placed in your personnel file. **Should unsatisfactory performance recur within the next 12 months, further action will be taken up to and including termination of employment.**

Please recognize the seriousness of this message and feel free to discuss questions or concerns with your Supervisor, Manager, or the Director of Human Resource while we work together to get your performance back on track.

Employee Comments: *(use additional sheets as necessary)*

Your signature is intended only to acknowledge receipt of the notice; it does not imply agreement or disagreement. Your signature implies understanding that this document will be placed in your personnel file.

Employee:	Date:
Immediate Supervisor:	Date:
Department Manager:	Date:
Human Resources:	Date:
☐ A copy of this document has been provided to the employee.	
Date:	Supervisor Initials:

Chapter 9

Measuring Performance to Spot Problems Early

Now that we know better, we must do better.
—Dr. Maya Angelou

In past years, most supervisors used one way to measure their employees' performance on the job. They did this by measuring how busy everyone stayed and the hours they put in on the job. Did people clock in and clock out on time; how much time did they stay after official work hours? Were people serious about their work and not having any fun? When employees had fun on the job, bosses thought that this suggested a lack of performance and productivity. It was once believed that no one could have fun at work and still be productive. Fun was just a sign of workers goofing off. Of course, those were the days when managers had an assembly-line mentality and used fear as their primary motivational tool for productivity.

WHAT WE CAN LEARN FROM LUCY AND ETHEL IN THE CANDY FACTORY (CIRCA 1952)

There's probably no better example of this type of supervision and performance measurement than in the *I Love Lucy* video clip from 1952, called "Job Switching" (CBS Fox Video), or sometimes better known as "Lucy and Ethel in the Candy Factory." Find this video clip on YouTube, and watch it so that you can explain the connection described here to your leaders. Better yet, show it to your leaders!

Lucy and Ethel get jobs wrapping chocolates in a candy factory. The candy factory supervisor is as tough as nails and shows little or no compassion for her new hires. Using fear as motivation to get as much productivity out of Lucy and Ethel as possible, the supervisor loudly barks the following orders, "All right girls, if one candy gets past you on this conveyer belt and into the packing room unwrapped, you're fired!" Believe it or not, this approach was once one of the most common methods used in measuring a worker's performance.

Motivated by fear that they would lose their jobs, Lucy and Ethel panic when the candy conveyer belt starts moving faster. They can't possibly wrap candy that fast. Knowing that the number of candies wrapped before passing into the packing room is how they will be measured, Lucy and Ethel resort to any and all means in order not to get fired when they hear their supervisor approaching.

The rest is comedy history and quite funny to watch when Lucy and Ethel begin stuffing the unwrapped chocolates down their uniforms and into their mouths. What's not so funny is that sheer panic and stressed behavior by employees who are about to undergo traditional performance evaluations still exists in organizations today.

PERFORMANCE AND PROBLEM-SOLVING DIAGNOSTIC TOOL KIT TO HELP YOU SPOT AND HANDLE PROBLEMS EARLY ON

This is a fast and easy-to-use 12-step diagnostic tool kit that will help guide you to examining and correcting problems facing your department, team, or organization. The process uses basic statements and questions that, when posed to employees, often bring to the surface the real performance issue at hand and, therefore, a possible solution.

Define a performance challenge or problem that you may find yourself facing, such as: Do my employees really have the training or knowledge they need to do the job right? Is there a better process than the one we are now using? Are my employees facing obstacles I am unaware of?

Once you've identified your employees' problems or challenges, select the most appropriate statement or questions from this tool kit to help further uncover a troubling issue and, thereby, get to the bottom of the matter. Let these phrases and questions further help you to analyze the underlying problem that may be at hand. As a result, you'll be wasting less time. Remember, smart leaders don't presume to have all the answers. Instead they ask smart questions and use tool kits like this one for documenting performance problems.

1. *Stop wasting time.* Get to the heart of the matter. Be direct. Start by asking, "What is the problem?"
   a. What is the difference between what is being done and what is expected?
   b. Describe your proof.
   c. How reliable is your proof?

2. *Performance discrepancies.*
   a. Are they important? How so?
   b. What happens if we do nothing?
   c. Is it even worth taking time to make the problem better?

3. *Performance problems resulting from lack of skill.*
   a. Could the performers do the job if their lives depended on their doing it correctly?
   b. Evaluate skills. Are they even adequate, or are they below adequate?

4. *Evaluating past performance.* Has it been better? When? What were the commonalities?
   a. Have current employees forgotten what they were trained to do?
   b. Do people know what is expected of them?

5. *Mastering skills by using them frequently.*
   a. Do employees get regular feedback on how they are doing?
   b. How is the way people are doing communicated to them?
   c. Do employees like the way in which they are provided feedback?

6. *Better ways to do things.* Is there another process that will get the job done?
   a. Would a better job description be useful?

b. Can employees relearn the task by watching others?

c. Can the process be changed or improved in some way?

7. *Having what it takes to be successful at doing the job.* What does it take?

   a. Is the physical and/or mental potential of the people involved strong enough?

   b. Are people truly qualified?

8. *Performance and punishment.* Is performance being punished?

   a. What is in it for the employee to do it right?

   b. Is doing the job somehow self-punishing?

   c. Is there a reason not to perform well?

9. *When not doing the job gets rewarded.*

   a. Have there been rewards in the past for doing the job wrong?

   b. Does doing it wrong draw attention to the worker?

   c. Do employees worry less, have less anxiety and tension, or get less tired if they do less work?

10. *Doing it right matters.*

    a. Is there a favorable outcome for doing it right?

    b. Are there consequences for not doing it right?

    c. Is there pride in doing the job?

    d. Is there any status or lack of it connected with the job?

11. *Obstacles to high performance.*

    a. Do employees know what is expected?

    b. Do employees know when it is expected?

    c. Is competition making the job too difficult?

    d. Are time and tools available?

    e. Is the job physically a mess and disorganized?

12. *Limitations on possible solutions.*

    a. Are there solutions that would be considered unacceptable to the organization?

    b. Do leaders have preferred solutions? Are they open to suggestions for improvement by workers?

    c. Can the organization afford the time and resources to find real solutions to real problems?

Once you've practiced using this tool kit, you will most likely find this to be a fast and easy technique that you'll refer to again and again for spotting potential problems early on. It will help you bring out the best in your workforce.

REEVALUATING CURRENT PERFORMANCE MEASUREMENT TOOLS

The information in this chapter will give you an opportunity to reevaluate your organization's performance measurement tools. Is there room for improvement? Will your organization allow your leaders to step outside the box, or must they adhere to the traditional performance review forms and formulas the organization has used for years?

Either way, the measurement tools and techniques you will find in this chapter will help you to open the door for creative and innovative thinking when you are training your leaders on the importance of measurement.

In his book *Out of Crisis* (MIT Press, 1982), Dr. W. Edwards Deming said the following of annual ratings:

> In practice, annual ratings are a disease, annihilating long-term planning, demolishing teamwork, nourishing rivalry and politics, leaving people bitter, crushed and bruised, battered, desolate, despondent, unfit for work for weeks after receipt of rating, and unable to comprehend why they are inferior.

This does not mean that a number system used for annual ratings in an organization cannot be effective. It can be. However, how that system is used and implemented and how it is backed up with, or supported by, various "performance building" opportunities and tools for people to use and improve and grow is where things become pivotal. If you are going to use a numerical grading system in your organization's annual reports and reviews, then it is important to ensure that the grading system provides a humanistic way of measuring ongoing performance development and includes coaching and employee development planning in the process. Improve on what you have now. Make it better. Take the time to upgrade your systemic approach to performance improvement.

HOW LEADERSHIP IN ORGANIZATIONS CAME TO USE PERFORMANCE EVALUATIONS

Almost 70 years ago, North America became intrigued with and energized by the concept and application of annual performance evaluations and reviews. The idea was that if managers reviewed an employee every six months or every year based on some sort of pre-determined criteria, in theory, employees would receive their rating and then use this feedback to improve their performance. In other words, it was believed, and still is in many organizations, that this was a tool that would make employees better. Unfortunately, that was not always the case.

The Impact of a Performance Review

The following is a true story shared by a manager who refuses to use the traditional approach when evaluating his employees:

> I remember when I was coming up through the ranks in this company. During one of my first evaluations, I only got a satisfactory rating for performance. I think my supervisor graded me a number three on the inane number scale that was used to rate my performance from one to five. I was devastated. Not only did the appraisal squash my confidence, but it took the air out of my sails and slowed my go-get-'em stride. The review haunted me, and I eventually left the department because of it.
>
> —Anonymous Manager

THE TRAUMA OF PERFORMANCE REVIEWS

In most organizations, performance reviews are conducted during the same time of year, over a period of a few weeks. During this time the entire organization can experience extreme trauma. Not only are leaders preparing themselves for conducting the painful assessments, but the anticipation of how employees will or won't respond can be agonizing. In addition, most employees wind up feeling demoralized and hiding their hurt feelings or anger. How do employees explain to their family that they received low ratings at their job? It's humiliating at the very least.

So what happened to the original idea of using performance evaluations as a method of improving the workforce? Are there ways to measure an organization's performance through its people and have it be an exhilarating and beneficial experience? The answer is yes, and it's called "praise in progress" and requires checking in frequently with people. This is how leaders achieve small wins and avoid potentially hazardous employee performance problems.

CONTINUOUS IMPROVEMENT VERSUS EMBARRASSMENT

The aim of leaders, when it comes to measuring performance, is not to get workers to try to become number one. Rather, the goal should be to encourage all workers to continually improve themselves. The leader who relies on evaluating talent on an annual basis via the traditional performance review is missing the point. After all, shouldn't a leader be a coach, not a judge? That means coaching and developing by using praise and feedback over time, not waiting for a year to give people the tools they need to improve themselves.

> The goal of measuring performance is not to get workers to try to become number one, thus competing with one another. Rather, the goal should be to get all workers to continually improve themselves and move toward departmental, organizational, and personal development and achievement.

IT STARTS WITH HIRING THE RIGHT PEOPLE

Leadership entails selecting the right people to do the job to begin with. Once the leaders hire those people, it is their responsibility to effectively orient them to the company and continually educate and train them so that they can master their jobs. In other words, the measurement and evaluation process is ongoing. In addition rather than being judgmental, it should be supportive and sustaining.

Tip

Avoid using figures to rank people unless the figures are used to determine a percentage of growth and learning in a specific skill area, like writing or listening. This way the numbers are not representative of the person's ability, but of a specific skill area that is being developed. Even then, the figures should be assigned by the employee and not determined by the employee's leader when possible. If you must use a numerical system, then enhance that system with critical employee development and coaching techniques that are provided for you in this book. Adapt, delete, modify, and expand on the tools you find here.

THE ORGANIZATION'S SYSTEM PRODUCES ITS BEHAVIORS

Using numbers as ratings when measuring an employee's performance only serves to point out the employee's faults and personalizes the rating, instead of focusing on the issues at hand. When you think about it, how can a behavior trait be changed through a scoring process? It can't be. It's the organization's system that produces behaviors. Change the system, and the behaviors will change, as well. Focusing on a numeric performance rating also enables the manager to "escape" talking with team members about behaviors and actual development. Numbers are "black and white"; behaviors are often shades of gray and require meaningful conversations and coaching.

MEASURING WHAT MATTERS IN THE REAL WORLD—A CASE STUDY PORTFOLIO

The old business maxim says, "What gets measured is what gets done." This statement is just as relevant as it ever was. Organizations today, no matter how creative and outside the box their performance is, still have to find ways to measure what's getting done and how much improvement is being made or needs to be made. You can bet someone is keeping score.

Following are some real-world measurement case studies that leaders can review to help them begin expanding their thinking when it comes to the many different ways leaders go about measuring an organization's performance. Examples provided include a business school, a high-tech manufacturer, and a start-up airline.

Ask your leaders to come up with their own new and effective ways to measure the performance of their departments or business units. Then have the leaders write their own case studies based on the format provided here. Ask the leaders this question: What are the measurements that matter most to you and why? Afterward, compile all the case studies and distribute them to all your leaders as a helpful addition to the following case study portfolio.

CASE STUDY 1

THE ORGANIZATION: LONDON BUSINESS SCHOOL, LONDON, ENGLAND

Goal: Have students be transformed by the experience of attending this institution of higher learning and be able to look back at the experience as life changing.

The London Business School was established in 1965 and serves thousands of graduate students and executives each year. Outside of the United States, it's ranked one of the top business schools in the world.

About a decade ago, then dean John A. Quelch announced that the school wasn't in the education business—it was in the transformation business. This, especially at the time, was a bold and innovative approach to higher-level learning at such a prestigious school.

In order to measure how the institution itself was doing, the school's leaders developed a tool called a transformational benchmarking questionnaire. This questionnaire is given to students who have taken a program or programs at the school. The survey asks questions such as: How much of the program that you took do you recall? Do you stay in touch with faculty? Do you stay in touch with fellow students? How big an impact has the program had on your career and on your quality of life?

How Results Are Measured

The school's survey is a vital tool for gathering important data, and leaders plan to have the survey administered as students' careers advance, including one year after they've left the school and then again every five years after that.

The results of these surveys provide detailed information regarding the performance of each student. Leaders at the London Business School then measure their performance against their objectives of creating a transformational experience for every student.

THE ORGANIZATION: SUN MICROSYSTEMS INC., PALO ALTO, CALIFORNIA

Goal: Sun systems are up and running at its customers' sites. Sun Microsystems calls this "system uptime."

With annual revenues in the billions of dollars, Sun Microsystems is one of the world's largest computer manufacturers. Sun has offices in 170 countries and provides end-to-end solutions for doing business in the network age. About a million developers use its Java programming language.

Behind the technology that put the dot in .com, Sun Microsystems is about innovation, but it's also about measuring performance from the way it designs and produces products to the way it creates value for shareholders. Leaders at Sun believe that an organization must closely align its ways of measurement with the ways that its customers measure. In other words, the measures that matter most to Sun are the measures that matter most to its customers.

To do this, Sun Microsystems compiles real-time feedback to monitor system uptime and downtime at its customers' sites. This tool provides instantaneous information, which is then used to determine what the causes of downtime might be. But that's not where the method of using real-time feedback stops. Information gathered is also used to train and educate people, to improve on existing processes, or to do whatever it takes to increase its customers' uptime so that Sun's customers, in turn, can maximize their own organization's ability to serve customers and clients. This system for measurement is supported by and cascades down from its top leadership to Sun's customers and its end users.

How Results Are Measured
Sun uses the following criteria to determine if it is performing to the best of its ability: Does the company understand the real needs of their customers?

And is it meeting those needs? It's the answers to these two questions that Sun believes have the biggest impact on its organization's performance.

THE ORGANIZATION: JETBLUE AIRWAYS CORPORATION, JOHN F. KENNEDY AIRPORT, NEW YORK

Goal: Provide the United States with the best low-fare, hassle-free, high-quality airline service it deserves by stressing values and a two-way commitment process between the airline and its people.

JetBlue, the most heavily capitalized start-up airline in aviation history, was poised from the start to bring to the New York metropolitan area a new brand of travel experience characterized by great service, cutting-edge technology, low fares, and great people.

Like other carriers, JetBlue closely measures what is called in airline lingo cost per available seat mile (CASM). In lay terms, how much does it cost to make a seat available for sale? That formula brings together every cost imaginable, like fuel, maintenance, and marketing. But, unlike some of its competition, JetBlue doesn't stop there when it comes to measuring its performance.

One of the measuring tools that has been used at the airline represents two-way employer/employee accountability and is referred to as JetBlue's two-way commitment. It starts in employee orientation with JetBlue's "commitment to you" and includes the following five criteria for measuring the airline's accountability to its employees:

1. We will have open, honest, and two-way communication always.
2. We will provide you with a work environment free from all forms of harassment.
3. You will have the opportunity to express your career aspirations and have them acted upon.
4. We will return your business-related phone calls within 24 hours.
5. We will provide you with the orientation training and proper tools to be successful in your job.

In return, employees are asked to sign a commitment. The statements in the employee commitment somewhat mirror JetBlue's commitment to its people and include the following criteria:

1. I will support and use JetBlue-sponsored training and education programs.

2. I will treat all customers for what they truly are: They are the very reason we exist.

3. I take care of and protect JetBlue assets.

4. I am completely honest in my communication with JetBlue employees.

5. I take personal responsibility for my decisions, actions, and professional growth.

Other helpful performance metrics include a monthly report to everyone in the company detailing 10 performance issues, such as how the airline is doing when it comes to lost baggage, on-time performance, and flight completion, to name a few.

How Results Are Measured

Twice a year employees of the airline will evaluate the company's leaders and their ability to live up to their commitments, just as employees themselves are evaluated by their supervisors.

The semiannual climate review is called the JetBlue quality of life survey and tells the airline's leaders how they're doing. In addition, the airline ties employee compensation at all levels to the results of how people execute the organization's values and commitments.

CHARACTERISTICS OF EFFECTIVE PERFORMANCE MEASUREMENT

Notice that the situation in each of the case studies meets the following 10 characteristics of effective performance measurement:

1. Relates to and supports the client's goals and objectives

2. Blends balance between people, customers, and the bottom line

3. Focuses on just a few important areas at one time

4. Indicates where performance can be improved

5. Indicates if training is needed

6. Is flexible and easy to revise if necessary

7. Aligns measurement with the organization's systems

8. Established by the people who are performing the jobs

9. Ensures the well-being of everyone in the organization

10. Tools and techniques translate strategy into action

Discuss with your leaders how the individual case studies they have written share these characteristics. Are there any gaps that need to be closed? Ask your leaders how they can use this list as a method to stay on track when establishing and creating their own performance metrics in the future.

PERFORMANCE BUILDERS

Help broaden your leaders' scope of awareness and sensitivity when it comes to measuring their employees' performance. Suggest to your leaders that rather than using an annual performance appraisal or review, they consider using, or adding onto their existing format, the following Performance Builder.

The Performance Builder is a powerful tool that your leaders can easily learn to use. It not only helps to build employees' performance, but it also builds their confidence, communications skills, vision, understanding, and accountability.

The great thing about using a Performance Builder is that it actually involves the employee in setting the standards by which he or she will be measured. Included in the Performance Builder is a valuable tool kit with self-scoring devices to help discern where an employee has seen measurable improvement, tools for measuring both personal and professional development, an experiential follow-up assignment for critical feedback from the field, and fast formulas for calculating return on investment.

How to Use the Performance Builder

Encourage your leaders to adapt the following format and tools to their needs, management style, business sense, and people skills. Remind them that everything is contextual. Your leaders cannot expect every technique and tool to work in every situation.

The objective of learning how to use this Performance Builder is so that your leaders will be better able to motivate others to perform at peak levels, while building a bridge between their employees' own interests and talents and the interests of the organization.

1. START BY DEFINING WHAT PERFORMANCE MEANS TO YOU AS A LEADER

Never assume that your employees will understand or know what it is you mean by performance. It is your responsibility as a leader to clearly define the term based on the circumstances of your organization. The word can take on a different meaning depending on whether you're manufacturing computers, selling software, marketing travel packages, or designing public relations materials.

Define your interpretation of performance here:

_____

_____

_____

2. TOGETHER WITH YOUR EMPLOYEE, ESTABLISH CLEAR AND SPECIFIC PERFORMANCE EXPECTATIONS

Invite discussion and encourage your employees to suggest their own parameters for measuring their performance. By doing this, you will be getting a good sense of what each employee believes is realistic.

As a leader, you, too, must share the standards of performance that you expect from a particular job. Characterize what you think is outstanding performance and what you consider to be unacceptable performance.

Research shows time and again that when employees are involved in their own performance measurement, they are more likely to accept and meet the challenge.

3. STRETCH YOUR EMPLOYEES AND HELP THEM BUY INTO IMPROVING PERFORMANCE

Employees buy into standards worthy of their time and energy. Getting employee buy-in isn't about creating a manipulative and compelling agenda. Consider performance measurement a joint venture and treat your employees like partners. When leaders do this, employees are more likely to be genuinely motivated to buy into the standards set for them and stretch themselves to reach higher performance levels. Remember, most employees want to take a role in raising their own performance expectations.

4. BE CLEAR ABOUT THE SCOPE OF RESPONSIBILITY YOU ARE GIVING

Be sure that your employee understands who exactly is responsible for what. When employees understand their responsibilities in relation to everyone else, the possibility of confusion is eliminated.

Help your employee plan to be spontaneous! This means that an employee's scope of responsibility may change at any time depending on unforeseen circumstances that may arise. Explain that adapting to unplanned situations is part of the employee's job and that when this happens, it's okay to broaden the scope of responsibility. But again, as the leader, you must be clear about what "broadening the scope of responsibility" means to you.

5. DOCUMENT WHAT'S BEEN AGREED ON

Documentation is a critical step in the Performance Builder. Create a written list of all the performance standards you and your employee have agreed upon. This will not be enough in guiding your employee to achieving success. Now you must be specific about what it's going to actually take to reach these expectations and attain these goals. You must document these steps as well and make this your employee's action plan.

Important note: Give a copy of this document to your employee and keep one for your file. At employee performance reviews, or whenever a project is completed, this document will serve you well as the platform from which agreed-upon standards of performance were measured.

6. FOLLOW-UP

As a leader it is essential that you make the time to observe and follow up with your employees on how things are going. Don't wait until the next review to check in with your employees to see how they're doing. Always observe and give feedback on jobs in progress. For less experienced employees, you might have to check in more often until they feel comfortable with their responsibilities.

7. OFFER "SPEEDBACK" AND REWARDS AND KEEP YOUR PROMISES

Be clear up front in the Performance Builder about what can be expected if the employee meets or exceeds the goals set (examples might include: money, special recognition such as an award certificate, day off, two-hour lunch break, more flexible work schedule, letter from the president, or more responsibility). Build in lots of small wins along the way too. Make recognition part of the plan. By doing this, you help your employees connect the reward with the behavior.

Also, the speed at which a leader responds to his or her people is important. Giving fast feedback will not only validate an employee's contribution but can ultimately determine his or her success. Try out these easy-to-use speedback tools from your Performance Builder tool kit when measuring and observing from a distance the continuous improvement of your people and their teams.

The following tool can be e-mailed, faxed, or even voicemailed to the appropriate person or team.

Remember: People just want to know where they stand. Speedback gives everyone an opportunity to calibrate where they are and anticipate and plan for what's coming next.

Speedback gives movement and momentum to every situation, without leaders needing to get caught up in long explanations and details. It doesn't bog down the communication process. It speeds up thinking and kicks idea-sharing up a notch.

Important note: Remember to always keep your promises. Never make a promise without a plan to deliver on that promise.

Speedback Template

Fast! Give us an update! What's happening over there?
What's working?
Any frustrations?
Quick! E-mail, text, or tweet back to Judy Smith.

Speedback Template—Fast Feedback Tips

Fast praise in progress:

> "Super job, Kevin. The project is awesome!!"

Fast empathy and understanding:

> "That really sounds frustrating, Mark. I can certainly see why you feel the way you do. I've come across something I think might help. When can we talk?"

Fast corrective action:

> "Hold everything! I love your enthusiasm, Linda, but I think you might want to try another approach. I'd like to share my experience with you on this, and I'd like to hear your thoughts."

Fast update:

> "Although I still don't have all the details, I thought you'd like a quick update on the information I have so far. Here it is."

Fast follow-up:

> "It's important that we follow up on this, Janice. Let's set a day and time to go over your progress."

8. PROVIDE YOUR EMPLOYEES WITH THE NECESSARY TRAINING AND RESOURCES TO BE SUCCESSFUL

According to management guru Peter Drucker, one of the secrets to IBM's earlier success was that the organization trained and trained and trained. When it comes to performance building techniques, training and employee development should be top of mind. Focus your training on employee needs. Ask employees what they need to learn. Don't arbitrarily decide that for them. And be sure to deliver training "just in time." This means getting training to people as close as possible to the time they need it.

Give your employees the critical measurement tools that will bolster their confidence and provide valuable feedback to the organization regarding its investment in training. Measure how effectively training is being used in the field and on the job with tools, like an experiential follow-up assignment.

Following are some additional measurement tools from your tool kit.

Personal Development Scorecard

Use the following tool as a template to help employees self-measure ongoing improvement. Remember, using figures to score a skill area is acceptable because it is a reflection on the performance skill and not on the person.

Also, using figures in this example works because employees score themselves. Using numbers on a scale of one to ten makes it easy to quickly assess measurable improvement in percentages. When we are able to offer upper-level management percentages like these, we are able to more easily assign a dollar value to their significance, providing easy-to-track return on investment.

Measurable Performance Improvement Tool

Personal Development Scorecard

This personal development scorecard will help employees to quickly and easily measure their own individual performance development and improvement in specific areas.

The scorecard is designed as a useful tool to gauge growth and identify areas in which additional improvement and development may be required. The best part is that the employees are the ones doing the grading; therefore, the use of a number system is acceptable.

The number 1 is lowest in rating, and the number 10 is highest in rating.

Skill Set	My Prior Grade	My Grade After	Percentage of Measurable Improvement*
Sample: Creative thinking as a manager	7	10	30%
Creative thinking as a manager			
Brain mapping			
Problem solving			
Stronger decision making			
Turbo charging the work environment			
Becoming an effective catalyst			
Understanding the lightning-in-a-bottle concept and thunderbolt thinking			
Getting unstuck from the rut and communicating better			
Motivating myself and influencing others			

(continued on next page)

Skill Set	My Prior Grade	My Grade After	Percentage of Measurable Improvement*
Kicking productivity and performance up a notch			
Building better teams			
Using new tools and techniques as a manager			
Authentic coaching and facilitating other people's success			
Competencies in the workplace			
Empowerment and delegation skills			
Building relation-ships as a manager			
Conflict solution finding			
*Note: It is recognized that there are variations in percentages using tens. The formula is rounded off to the nearest full percentage point for ease of use and flexibility.			

The 90-Day Mailback Worksheet

After completing the mailback worksheet like the one provided on the following page, have employees fold the worksheet down to a number 10-size envelope and have them address the envelopes to themselves. Be sure they all seal their worksheet with tape or a sticker. Collect the worksheets and create a tickler file or mark your calendar to mail back everyone's worksheets in 90 days.

The impact this will have on employees is substantial and becomes an honest self-measurement tool on whether or not they stayed on task regarding their goals and objectives. If they did, that's great, and employees will gain a sense of satisfaction from knowing they followed through. If they did not, there's still no harm done. No one else will have seen the worksheet. However, it will certainly serve as a hard-hitting reminder of what that employee failed to complete. You'll be surprised at the positive feedback you will receive after you have mailed back these worksheets to your employees.

The Experiential Follow-Up Assignment

Measuring what employees learn in a training classroom is one thing. Measuring how effective those lessons are in the real world is another thing entirely. The follow-up assignment, such as the one provided on page 225, provides leaders with the hard-core results of how employees are actually applying the training techniques and lessons they learned. The feedback this measurement tool brings to management will be extremely helpful in justifying training time and expense. It takes training costs and turns them into a justified training investment.

90-Day Mailback Worksheet

Instructions

This worksheet is confidential and for your use only. In the space provided below, record the personal and professional goals you will work toward regarding further development of the skills you have learned in this training program.

To help you keep on track and stay focused on your goals and objectives, this worksheet will serve as a helpful reminder of the things most important to you that you would like to accomplish and work toward. When you have completed this worksheet, fold it, place it into the envelope provided, and seal it. Address the envelope to yourself. This mailback worksheet will be collected in class and mailed to you in 90 days.

Skills that I would like to improve on and develop over the next 90 days, include the following:

_____

_____

_____

_____

_____

_____

_____

_____

My personal plan of action to work toward ongoing personal development of these skills, will include doing the following:

_____

_____

_____

_____

_____

_____

_____

Experiential Follow-Up Assignment and Measuring Tool for Personal Growth and Professional Development

The outcome of this on-the-job exercise will be to measure the effectiveness and results of the new skills you have learned since completing this training program. Attach additional sheets of paper if necessary.

1. What specific skills outlined in your mailback worksheet can you now apply on the job?

    _____

    _____

    _____

    _____

    _____

2. Describe a real-world situation that you have been able to handle more effectively as a result of this information. What was the challenge? How did you use the skills you learned in class? What were the results?

    _____

    _____

    _____

    _____

    _____

3. What tools, tips, or techniques learned have you been able to quickly reference and apply since completing this training program?

    _____

    _____

    _____

    _____

    _____

Note: Please complete this tool as an experiential follow-up assignment and return it to your supervisor, _____, no later than 30 days from today's date.

9. HELP EMPLOYEES CALCULATE RETURN ON INVESTMENT

Help your employees understand how to quickly calculate return on investment (ROI) when it comes to offering solutions to problems or requesting more money to handle a specific challenge in their department. When employees come closer to thinking like their leaders by first determining what it's going to take to make something happen and whether it's worth it, their contribution to the bottom line becomes evident and will build confidence in the team's overall recommendations to management.

10. EXPECT THE BEST FROM YOUR EMPLOYEES AND DON'T BE SURPRISED IF THAT'S WHAT YOU GET

Research shows that a leader's expectations of others directly affect an organization's productivity and profitability. As a leader, you will get better performance from your people if that's what you expect of them. Our expectations of others influence their behavior. When a leader tells his or her employees upfront what performance standards are expected of them, those workers achieve higher levels of performance as a result.

THE ART OF MEASUREMENT

Perhaps what gets measured is what gets done—but what gets measured is also what gets learned, becomes habit, and gets reinforced.

Use this chapter to guide your leaders in learning and using new and powerful performance measurement techniques that fit their special circumstances. Some tools may work better in certain situations, while others may take special adapting or customization in order to work in your organization. Measuring performance has actually become somewhat of an art that is mastered over time and with experience.

LEADER'S CHECKLIST FOR MEASURING PERFORMANCE

Use the following checklist to review the 10 critical steps in your leaders' Performance Builder:

1. Define what performance means to you as a leader.
2. Together with your employees, establish clear and specific performance expectations.
3. Stretch your employees, and help them buy into improving performance.
4. Be clear about the scope of responsibility you are giving to employees.
5. Document what's been agreed on.
6. Follow up.
7. Offer "speedback" and rewards. Keep your promises.
8. Provide your employees with the necessary training and resources to be successful.
9. Help employees calculate return on investment.
10. Expect the best.

10 CHARACTERISTICS OF EFFECTIVE PERFORMANCE MEASUREMENT

Do your leaders' metrics meet the characteristic criteria for performance measurement? Use this checklist to be sure:

1. Relates to and supports the client's goals and objectives
2. Blends balance between people, customers, and the bottom line
3. Focuses on just a few important areas at one time
4. Indicates where performance can be improved
5. Indicates if training is needed
6. Is flexible and easy to revise if necessary
7. Aligns with the organization's systems

8. Is developed by the people who are performing the jobs

9. Ensures the well-being of everyone in the organization

10. Translates strategy into action

DISCUSSION STIMULATORS

Here are some questions that can bring about a candid discussion regarding performance appraisal and evaluation:

1. Can you think of a time when you had a performance appraisal conducted on you that you considered to be unfair and that made you feel incompetent or unappreciated?

2. What is the goal of measuring performance?

3. Why is it valuable for employees to be able to calculate return on investment?

4. What are the benefits of a leader using a Performance Builder as opposed to a traditional performance evaluation, or in conjunction with an existing review process?

THE KEY TO HIGH-PERFORMANCE TEAMS

As we have outlined in this chapter, there are many ways to measure employee performance. It is important for leaders to "think outside the box" about how to evaluate how each team member is doing against objectives. The annual performance review is just one way to review performance, and quite often it is an ineffective way. We have given you several tools and strategies that allow you to engage team members and make performance evaluation a core part of your day-to-day interaction and not just an annual event. This is key to creating a high-performing team.

Chapter 10

Using the Strategies Successfully in Your Organization

How can you use and leverage the tools, practices, and strategies presented in the previous chapters? We suggest that you "start from where you are," but use a helicopter view of where you want to go. In other words, rise above what you have and look at the big picture in life. Regardless of whether you are a leader or HR partner, or both, be honest about the capabilities you or the target audience have and introduce the tools that best fit the skill level and situation. Meet the users where they are and then help them and you get to where you want to be.

But getting to where you want to go and ensuring a smooth ride along the way requires alignment. Just like the wheels on your car—if the wheels are out of alignment, the ride to where you are going is likely to be bumpy rather than smooth. It's the same in life. Life and careers are more challenging when parts of our life are out of sync.

Studies show over and over again that personal life issues often create employee performance problems.

Helping your employees to be in harmony with their "whole person" can make the difference between a dysfunctional workplace and a productive, high-performing workplace. When we say "whole person," we are suggesting that you encourage your organization's leadership to be mindful of a whole-person approach to solving problems and growing talent.

No longer can organizations afford to compartmentalize their employees' lives. Drawing an invisible line that suggests a worker leave his or her personal life at the door when on the job ignores every aspect of humanness. In today's global workplace, that line is outdated and blurred. We know it is impossible for an employee to close off his or her personal life when coning to work because such behavior goes against human nature. One dimension of a person's life is affected by all others, and both the professional and personal lives of employees are closely connected.

As a leader, it's your responsibility to help navigate turbulent times and rough patches along the way.

And just like being lost in the forest, or at sea, having a compass to help guide the way can be critical.

FINDING PERFORMANCE IMPROVEMENT

In every organization there comes a time when leadership development must rise up and meet the needs of its people. Ralph Waldo Emerson's often quoted "our chief want is someone who will inspire us to be what we know we can be" seems fitting for any one of us who has faced the challenge of developing and coaching employees to a higher level of potential and talent. Guess what? That's you. The person reading this book and trying a variety of new approaches, tips, tools, and innovative techniques gleaned from this book. You're the one Emerson is describing in this quote—not just an HR professional or leader (manager, supervisor, business owner, etc.). Here's the turning point where you get to reframe your job description. Here's where you kick things up a notch and get in alignment with the bigger picture. Start thinking of yourself as a:

- Developer of extraordinary leadership
- Excavator of exceptional talent
- High-performance problem solver and innovative solution finder

- Architect of turbo-charged, high-performance teams
- Chief navigator of bringing out the best in people

You get the idea.

IT TAKES A WHOLE-PERSON APPROACH TO FIND EQUILIBRIUM

All the templates, tools, tips, and techniques in this book, or in the world for that matter, won't mean anything if you can't show employees how to activate their talents, competencies, skill sets, unique personalities, contributions, and creative ideas, and you need to figure out a balanced approach to doing it. This is a process that is in alignment with the *whole-person approach* to employee development we discussed earlier.

Try using this employee performance and balance assessment tool to get started. Encourage employees to use areas for needed improvement as discussion stimulators and to use areas of strength to mentor and coach others along the way. This tool should be used at least every six months, as core competencies and areas of needed improvement will shift and require ongoing calibration.

This performance tool will help you to find balance and equilibrium to build your self-confidence, one step at a time, in one specific area of your life at a time. Its purpose is to help you to measure the equilibrium in your life. The tool provides a fast overview of the areas in which you are steadily improving and others that need more attention in order for you to gain greater self-confidence and the peace of mind we all need for greater personal and professional development and happiness.

On a scale of 1 to 10, with 10 representing confidence and competency in one area, circle the number on the compass that best corresponds with where you are in your life right now. After you have circled a number for each area, draw a line around the compass by connecting each number. The goal is to work toward having, at the highest number possible, the smoothest line and a connection to each area around the compass. This tool will give you immediate

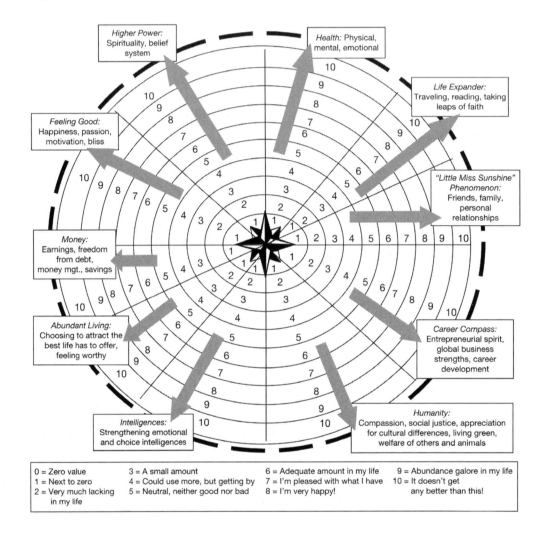

0 = Zero value	3 = A small amount	6 = Adequate amount in my life	9 = Abundance galore in my life
1 = Next to zero	4 = Could use more, but getting by	7 = I'm pleased with what I have	10 = It doesn't get
2 = Very much lacking in my life	5 = Neutral, neither good nor bad	8 = I'm very happy!	any better than this!

feedback on the areas in which you are riding along smoothly and feeling confident with a strong self-image, and the areas in which you may be experiencing some bumpiness and lower self-esteem.

We have learned from working with leaders that addressing most challenges starts with a straightforward gap analysis. You accomplish this by identifying the current state and by then articulating the desired state. You must then develop an action plan to address the gap between the two.

Solving performance problems fits this simple gap analysis model. Refer to the four-step model outlined in Chapter 1.

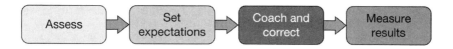

By assessing the performance situation, you identify the current state. Without this information a leader takes the chance of assuming and/or acting on partial or incorrect information. Setting performance expectations articulates the desired state. Coach and correct and measure results are the action plan to get you to the desired state.

MANAGING PERFORMANCE IN YOUR SPECIFIC CULTURE

Each organization, function, and department has a unique performance culture. Each leader defines and measures performance a little differently; even within the same performance management system.

Leaders need to be aware of both their performance management philosophy and their management style; that is, how they carry out that philosophy. Many times leaders manage performance without much thought. They are focused on getting the job done and holding employees accountable for assignments and policy compliance. This approach can create a vacuum of sorts and raises several questions and challenges. Is the leader in sync with the company performance culture?

Human resources often plays a large role in educating leaders about both the performance management process and the performance culture. This is done through several channels and should start at the beginning of the leader's tenure—when he or she is either new to the company or has been promoted to a leadership role.

The orientation/onboarding/transition program is a perfect place to start educating leaders about the organization's performance management philosophy and process. As mentioned in Chapter 1,

Performance Culture

Answers to the following questions define a performance culture:

- What behaviors, skills, and strengths does the company reward and recognize, formally and informally?
- How is performance assessed?
- What role do employees play in the performance assessment?

It is important for leaders to understand the performance culture and make a conscious decision to map their style based on the culture.

the three core components of an onboarding plan are: knowledge, relationships, and feedback. Part of knowledge is gaining an understanding of the company's core talent management processes, such as performance management. The leader's HR partner can educate as well as incorporate the specifics of the leader's team into the knowledge building. Once leaders have an understanding of the performance culture and process, leaders should then meet with team members to discuss performance management and how they interpret and use the performance management process. This goes beyond the annual review process and includes performance evaluation and a discussion of what constitutes a higher level of performance.

Our coauthor Brenda Hampel once served as a director of HR at a large pharmaceutical services company and had a team of seven direct reports—some of whom she had chosen for the team and others she inherited. Here she describes what it is like:

As part of my plan for selecting and building my team, I talked with each of the candidates and team members about our company's performance management process, as well as how I understand and apply the performance measurements and integrate our department goals and objectives. This discussion also gave me the opportunity to talk about my management style, how I prefer to keep up on progress of projects, as well as what and how I will hold each team member accountable. This discussion got all of us on the same page and gave managers a road map to apply with their direct reports.

We eliminated any misperceptions and/or assumptions that team members may have and allowed us to truly focus on performance.

PUTTING THE STRATEGIES IN ACTION

Once more, HR subject-matter expert Stephanie Montanez demonstrates specific ways you can put your strategies for performance improvement into action in the real world. Montanez asks that her managers develop mini case studies that include the following components for measurement:

1. Case study topic
2. Identify the performance issue
3. Action taken
4. Results achieved
5. Final remarks for follow-up

According to Montanez, when leaders take the time to case study a real-life scenario, everyone learns from the experience and a field guide of sorts is developed for future reference and for training new hires in the HR division of any company.

Here, Montanez shares six case studies that fit her recommended format. She recommends that you adapt and modify these examples to fit your own organization's or department's specific needs.

CASE STUDY 1

EMPLOYEE TARDINESS AND BEGINNING TO FAIL MONTHLY AUDITS OF WORK PERFORMANCE

Susan had been with the company for a few months and had started out well. After a few months, she began calling in sick more and more often, and when she did come in to work, she had started coming in late—missing her beginning work time. This resulted in a verbal warning from her supervisor for her tardiness and attendance issues. In addition to this, Susan started to fail audits that she was normally passing each month. Employees are required to have audits done on their efficiency each month and must have a minimum of 95 percent accuracy. Susan's performance had dropped below this number for three consecutive months.

Identify the Performance Issue

Her supervisor noted that this was out of character for Susan, so she decided to bring Susan in to her office to have a conversation regarding her concerns that continued occurrences, tardiness, and failed audits could result in further disciplinary action. Her supervisor explained her concern on Susan's change in behavior, asking that, as her manager, was there any assistance that she could offer in the area of training, time management, or even whether a schedule change to start at a later time would help.

Susan explained to her supervisor that she was going through a difficult time. The supervisor offered Susan the Employee Assistance Program information that was offered by the company. This could help her resolve personal issues through counseling. The supervisor also offered a time-management schedule to help Susan to focus on her daily tasks while at work. Susan received this information positively and agreed that she was indeed starting to fall behind. She thanked her supervisor and said she would try to do better.

Action Taken

Together, the supervisor and Susan came up with a plan: They would change her schedule to allow her more time in the morning to get her children to school and day care. They developed a time management schedule to help Susan focus on her daily tasks. This schedule outlined specific time frames to work on each daily task. The supervisor was there to help her on a daily basis. Susan also started auditing her own work every day. By self-auditing her work, Susan started passing her audits again. Susan revealed to her supervisor that she found she was making mistakes before because she was not focusing on the work at hand. She thanked her supervisor for stepping in and giving her a concrete way to be successful.

Results

Susan's supervisor saw immediate improvement in attendance, having moved her start time from 8:00 a.m. to 8:30 a.m. each day. In the area of staying on task, her supervisor was able to see improvement over the next few weeks, as Susan began to use the time management schedule. Using this technique, Susan was not falling behind any more in accomplishing her daily work. Her audits improved as well, and she passed her next monthly audit with flying colors. Her audits are now touching on 100 percent accuracy consistently. Susan has, in fact, increased her production and performance on the job. She is no longer calling in sick and is on time to work every day. She is still with the company and is a contributing member of the team.

Final Remarks from Her Supervisor

I think the best way to encourage employee performance improvement is by listening. This way you can find out what the true nature of the problem is and then address it together with the employee.

VIOLATION OF SEXUAL HARASSMENT POLICY

Cindy had been an employee for over a year with the company. She had violated the company's sexual harassment policy several times. Out of all the employment policies, sexual harassment can be the one policy that can land an employer in hot water if it is not investigated and properly rectified immediately. Once the policy infringement came to the notice of her supervisor, that supervisor took immediate action.

Identify the Performance Issue

Once her supervisor received the formal complaint about Cindy's behavior, the supervisor investigated it immediately. After the supervisor completed the investigation, it was found that the complaint was true and factual. At that time the supervisor did not feel that the infraction was significant enough to terminate Cindy's employment. The supervisor issued a second written warning with an action plan of improvement. Cindy told her supervisor that she understood this action, and that she would not violate that particular policy again. She vowed to follow company policies from then on.

Action Taken

Several months later, Cindy's supervisor received another complaint about similar behavior. She issued Cindy a final written warning and had another serious conversation with Cindy, stating that any additional incidents would result in immediate termination of employment. Cindy stated that she understood this.

A few months later, her supervisor received a third complaint about similar behavior. The supervisor felt that the infraction was serious enough to warrant immediate termination of employment. The supervisor went to the HR manager, who decided to take a risk: instead of sending Cindy on her way, the HR manager asked another supervisor to take Cindy under her wing and to mentor her. The new supervisor knew that Cindy was a skilled worker and decided to undertake the challenge of mentoring her. This new supervisor worked closely with Cindy (including individual mentoring and coaching) to help her develop her people skills, with the understanding that this was Cindy's last chance to remain with the company. Cindy was given a performance management form that was used to outline corrective action. Cindy's goal was to not receive any additional complaints from coworkers, and that she could not retaliate against the other employees who had filed the complaints. Additionally, she must follow all company policies.

Results

Over the next two years, Cindy gradually improved her people skills and thrived in her new environment under her new supervisor's tutelage. Cindy has exhibited new confidence and has learned more about her work, becoming an expert in her new department. Cindy has been promoted to a supervisory position herself and has had to coach other employees to follow company policies and procedures. This is her way of "paying it forward."

Final Remarks from Her Supervisor

Cindy's promotion was such a success story—it is one that we can definitely say mentoring and coaching was worth the time and effort. When employees

---

To improve employee performance, several things need to happen:

- You need to provide the employee with a work environment that grows talent and wants to train, develop, and mentor the staff to reach higher levels of performance.

- You need to have an employee with the proper aptitude for learning and a positive attitude to accept constructive feedback. Such an employee can then take that feedback, run with it, and improve.

- Employees should not make excuses on why they cannot meet their goals and objectives. Instead, they should set new goals to hit each week (or month) for continuous improvement.

- The employee and the leader need to meet regularly to make sure that good performance is measured, with movement and momentum toward meeting and exceeding goals.

- You should provide employees with a mentoring plan, learning resources, and regular training (we use an employee development coach for this purpose).

realize that they have an opportunity, and then are willing to take that opportunity, along with a management staff willing to coach—it is a win-win situation. I believe that Cindy will continue to grow and mentor others.

CASE STUDY 3

EMPLOYEE IS TECHNICALLY STRONG, PROMOTED TO MANAGEMENT POSITION WITHOUT "PEOPLE SKILLS"

Linda had great proficiency in her very technical position. She excelled in her job duties and was duly promoted to a supervisor position during her time with the company. The one thing she lacked was the softer skills—the "people skills" that are necessary to lead a team.

Identify the Performance Issue

The human resources department received several complaints from her team regarding her management style. They said Linda was "unapproachable, cynical, condescending, and too goal oriented" in speaking to them. The HR director determined what skills Linda needed to improve and set up some voluntary classes held in-house on leadership. The classes were conducted by the HR director and were designed to focus on communicating with other employees based on each person's individual personality.

Action Taken

The classes were held each week for four to five weeks. Each session lasted one hour, on a one-on-one basis, with the HR director providing the training. Linda was also given homework assignments each week to complete. This plan was oral and not formal, since none of the complaints about Linda were a violation of company policy. Had Linda not made positive steps to improve her communications with her team (and her team continued to not want to work for her), it may have led to a formal coaching plan for improvement.

Linda was very focused on learning new skills and took everything in a positive manner. She started to improve with her interpersonal communication with her team. Her team started reaching goals higher than company expectations. Linda was amazed at how people skills (no longer criticizing her team and demotivating them), along with her great technical skills, allowed her team to be very successful.

Results

The transformation was noticeable and almost immediate. Once Linda was aware of her deficiencies and was given the tools for success, she took the necessary steps to improve. Linda continued to improve and excel at work over the next year. She strived to learn more about her staff members—what made them tick—and took special care to motivate them and encourage them to greatness. Linda also volunteered for work groups and made many positive contributions to the company overall.

Linda continues to be a very active employee in the company and has been promoted into a management position. She now nurtures and assists her supervisors with their interpersonal skills to help them reach higher levels within their teams. This instance shows that mentoring and coaching a technically savvy employee with interpersonal skills pays off for all involved. Her team's productivity has increased by over 30 percent. Additionally, Linda's team started experiencing a lot of "good" turnover—meaning more than half of her staff was promoted into other positions.

Final Remarks from Her Supervisor

By playing to Linda's strengths (her strong work ethic, job duty know-how) and mentoring/coaching her in interpersonal matters, everybody gained a positive outcome. Linda's staff has proven to be an excellent team, and Linda, herself, has grown as a businessperson.

CASE STUDY 4

EMPLOYEE'S WORK PERFORMANCE NOT MEETING EXPECTATIONS

David was hired as a medical billing coder for the company. He did well in his training and was highly competent at his position at first. A few months into the job, his work began to suffer. His supervisor noticed that David's attitude had become defensive and defiant, and he was not open to receiving constructive feedback. This went on for a few months and resulted in oral and written warnings to improve his work performance to meet company standards.

Identify the Performance Issue

David's supervisor realized that there was more going on in David's life, leading to this destructive behavior. She invited David into her office and asked what was going on overall. David confided in her that he was going through a personal loss in his family and had a recent failed relationship that was troubling him. This situation was affecting his outlook on life and his job performance.

Action Taken

The supervisor told David that she and the other people in the office were there to support him—not to point out his work flaws. His supervisor stressed to David that she was not his enemy—she was there to help. She then suggested that David take ownership of his attitude and turn things around. David realized that his work was "the only stable thing in his life" and resolved to be more positive in the workplace. David's supervisor told him that she would help out in every way possible for him to be a success at his job. They had several coaching sessions over the next few weeks to help David turn things around.

Results

Within a few weeks, David started to change his attitude and behavior. His work became more balanced, and his competence improved 100 percent. His relationships with other coworkers and his supervisor improved greatly. With this improvement, David was able to accept a position that included specialized coding for worker's compensation services in all the states that the company handled. This is very detailed work, with each state's codes differing greatly. David was the only individual in his office to score 100 percent in numerous categories in his annual assessment. This led to an increase in pay and an increase in David's self-confidence. David continues to be a valuable member of the team.

Final Remarks from His Supervisor

Treat your employees as a whole person, not just a cog in the machine. If you can see the entire picture, you can help your employees work through challenges and become successful in their positions.

CASE STUDY 5

POOR (CONDESCENDING) MANAGEMENT STYLE WITH EMPLOYEES

Robert was a new supervisor who was not comfortable delegating duties to his team. The style he used was perceived as very condescending by his employees. The human resources department started receiving several complaints from Robert's staff, saying that he "spoke down" to them and treated them like children.

Identify the Performance Issue

Upon receiving these complaints, they were presented to Robert. Initially Robert did not believe that he was doing anything wrong and asked for specific feedback from the human resources department, which was provided. He was informed that he needed to improve his interpersonal and management skills in order to stay in his position. His resistance to change was affecting his department. His team continued to suffer, production decreased, absenteeism increased, and the complaints about his management style continued. Robert still did not believe that he was doing anything wrong and did nothing to improve his interpersonal communications.

Action Taken

The HR director, after seeing that there was no improvement, knew that there was going to have to be a formal action plan in the future for Robert. Even though he was a good employee, his position as a supervisor was at risk. At this point, another, nonsupervisory position opened up that Robert qualified for. The HR director encouraged Robert to accept this new position in order to ease the situation with his department.

Results

Robert took the new position and things turned around immediately. Robert's transfer to a position that did not require supervisory skills became his saving grace. He was able to use all of his previous skills and technical abilities, and continued to excel at work, and was awarded a "star award" at the end of the year. Robert was recently promoted to a higher position in the company. He now directs work flow for 80 employees, and uses his abilities to the fullest extent. He has changed from being a substandard supervisor to a successful, contributing employee in the company.

Final Remarks from His Supervisor

Sometimes, to improve performance, you have to look at your employees' skills and abilities and play to their strengths. Since Robert was technically sound, we felt he was just in the wrong position within the company. Once we found the correct position for him, he was able to improve and is now a very productive and skilled employee.

CASE STUDY 6

LANGUAGE—CULTURAL BARRIER AFFECTING MANAGERIAL PERFORMANCE

George was a great employee and was promoted to supervisor of his department. He was struggling with his interpersonal skills with his employees, due to a different cultural outlook on how to run a department. He also had trouble successfully communicating with his employees.

Identify the Performance Issue

George was originally from Russia. He had a very strict supervisory style, bordering almost on a military style of ordering his employees to do tasks. This did not go over well with his employees. He also had difficulty translating words from Russian to English, and many times the wrong word would be used. It was not his intention to offend his staff, but this invariably happened on a few instances. He was in charge of 15 employees, and the human resources department began to receive several complaints from his staff.

An example of miscommunication/understanding came from a newly hired employee. This employee had requested time off for her wedding, which was approved during the recruiting process. Once the employee was placed on George's team, she requested an additional week off for a honeymoon to Hawaii that was already paid in full (as a gift). George did not want to approve the time off, even with proof that the tickets and hotel fees had already been paid. His justification was that she had already requested some time off, and this was in excess of the initial request. The human resources department had to get involved, and facilitated getting her the additional time off through an unpaid personal leave of absence.

Action Taken

The HR director took some time to investigate the many complaints from George's staff. It was determined that George's demeanor and choice of words were not right for the workplace. Additionally the HR director determined that it was not George's intent to offend his employees—it was due to the language barrier and cultural differences. The HR director decided to work personally with George, to help him understand the differences. At first, George was a bit reluctant to accept this help, as he did not feel he was being overbearing, or using the wrong words. After he was provided with very specific feedback, he "got it" and was ready for help with his interpersonal and language skills. A member of the human resources department set up one-on-one meetings with George to assist him with his new goals of improving employee morale and setting up a clear way of communicating with his employees. George's manager also assisted in helping, by acting as a sounding board for George to talk to before meeting with his employees.

His manager also sat in on George's team meetings to offer feedback and advice, assisting in George's growth as a supervisor.

Results

This process took several months, but overall improvement took place. George decided that he wanted to use his accounting degree and applied for another supervisory position within the company that required his degree. He is now supervising a small group of highly skilled accounting employees and is running a very successful team. His self-confidence with the English language has improved immeasurably, and his team is much more understanding of what he is trying to convey in meetings. His team is top-notch, with a great attendance record, no turnover, and very high productivity.

Final Remarks from His Supervisor

With the proper training, and direct, immediate feedback, we were able to improve performance and provide additional opportunities for George. This is a win-win solution for the company.

CONCLUSION

We started this book by pointing out many of the reasons/excuses leaders give for not having performance discussions with their employees. We spent the remainder of the book providing strategies, resources, and tools to help leaders get past those reasons and excuses.

Many leaders are simply unaware of how or when to address performance challenges. They may even need help in defining and identifying the challenges. By creating a higher level of awareness of the leader's role, the performance bar can be raised for both leaders and their employees. The leader needs to set the expectations and hold the team members accountable; employees need to meet the expectations and comply with the policies and procedures of the organization.

By proactively managing performance, leaders and their teams can "pass go and collect $200" and focus on the fun stuff that is motivating and contributes to the department and company objectives and success.

We all remember Maslow's hierarchy of needs:

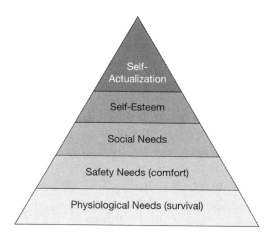

Think of managing performance as satisfying the basic needs. If we don't take care of the basic needs of employees, the employees are unable to reach their full potential.

Leaders who take responsibility for clearly communicating expectations, motivating team members, holding them accountable for results, rewarding them, and managing performance issues that arise build a strong, highly functioning team and leadership brand that inspires team members to reach their full potential.

THE REAL LEARNING BEGINS NOW

Start where you are today. Define where you want to go and then build a road map that integrates the strategies and resources we have shared with you to take you to your desired destination.

It is our hope that you will decide when using this book to take additional initiative to adapt, delete, modify, and expand on the examples provided. This is our formula for ongoing success, and we highly recommend it to every reader of this field guide. No one book can be, or ever will be, the end all or absolute answer to everyone's specific needs or concerns. The key and formula for your ongoing success will be to take the many templates, case studies, examples, models, ideas, suggestions, and real-world tips and tool kits in this book and make them better. We hold you responsible for breathing life into this document. It is your infusion of creativity and enthusiasm that will give this body of work depth and breadth.

In other words, the real learning and application of what's contained in this book begins *after* you've read it.

This is not just a how-to-do-things-better book; it's also a what-to-do-better book. It is your active involvement and additional ideas and ways to apply the material that will enhance the value of this resource tenfold. We ask that you please include and give your employees the opportunity to contribute their ideas to this enormous process. The combination of everyone's thoughts for new and better processes is something we can all benefit from greatly. In fact, the three of us invite you to share with us how you have taken ideas from this book and helped to make things better in your own organization. Visit our Web sites (www.AnneBruce.com and www.ConnecttheDots Consulting.com) and send us e-mails about your successes. We'd love to hear from you.

The next step is to help your employees to write and develop their own personal and professional employee development plans. To do this, check out Anne's book called *Perfect Phrases for Employee Development Plans* (McGraw-Hill, 2010), and Brenda and Erika's book, *Perfect Phrases for New Employee Orientation and Onboarding* (McGraw-Hill, 2011).

It is our hope that this book will serve you well as an ongoing and continuous leadership tool and field guide when the going gets tough—or better yet, before things get tough! It's no secret that we work in a time in which employee issues and performance problems are often unique, exhausting, and more challenging than ever for today's leaders and HR professionals. How you choose to equip yourself to handle these challenges is what will separate you from the flock and move you and your team forward in a positive and evolving direction. We're all in this together, traveling the same path toward the same destination—helping people to become their best! The three of us are more than pleased to know that you will be taking this book along with you on the journey.

Index

Abandonment, job, 94–95, 137
Absences:
    excessive, 102–103, 129–130
    from work area, 146
Accountability, 117–118
Active listening, 45–47
Alignment, 40–47
    gauging, 41–43
    improving, 46–47
    and performance dialogues, 43–46
Amazon.com, 47
American Express, 50
Angelou, Maya, 203
Angry outbursts, 145
Annoying habits, 142–143
Annual performance reviews, 204–207
Assessment:
    in four-step model, 27–28
    of team members, 111–114
Assumptions, 44–46
Attendance and tardiness problems, 100–105
    case study of, 235–237
    excessive absence, 102–103, 129–130
    excessive tardiness, 100–101
    FMLA abuse, 104–105

Baby boomers, 164, 165
Balanced style, 117
Behavior, focus on, 123
Behavior and conduct problems, 68–77
    angry outbursts, 145
    annoying habits, 142–143
    conflict between employees, 125–126
    inappropriate conversations with
        coworkers, 135
    inappropriate language, 68–69, 130–131
    interrupting and not listening, 150–151
    negativity about company policies,
        140–141
    not meeting minimum job requirements,
        70–71
    politically incorrect behavior, 74–75
    spreading gossip and rumors, 72–73,
        137–138
    talking inappropriately to coworkers, 135
    under the influence at work, 76–77,
        148–149

Best-in-class organizations, xiv–xv, 21, 39–40
    (*See also specific companies*)
Bezos, Jeff, 47
Boss, communicating with, 6–7
Boston Consulting Group, 59
Brand, leadership, 37
Branson, Sir Richard, 48, 55

Carbonara, Scott, 48–49, 51, 54–56, 58, 60,
    62, 63
Cell phone policy, 182–185, 188–189,
    192–193
Changes in processes, resistance to, 147–148
Check-ins, time-based, 46–47
Chism, Marlene, 156–159, 163
Clarity:
    in documenting problems, 118
    in Performance Builder, 217
    in setting expectations, 29
    and workplace drama, 156–157
Clinton, Bill, 57
Coaching, 108
    coaching and development plans, 170–201
    in four-step model, 30–31
    in proactive performance management,
        108–109
    when delegating tasks, 114
    (*See also* Employee Coaching and
        Development Plan)
Communication(s), 39–65
    for addressing drama, 156
    and alignment, 40–47
    assumptions in, 44–46
    at best-in-class organizations, xiv–xv, 39–40
    context in, 60, 61
    conversational, 57
    of expectations, 5–8
    feedback on, 63, 64
    high-intensity listening in, 62, 63
    ineffective, 50, 51
    intentional, 61
    interdepartmental, 7
    with new employees, 16–19
    nonverbal, 152–154
    proactive, 47–49
    repetition in, 58, 59
    in talent management cycle, xvi

247

Communication(s) *(continued)*:
  with team, 6
  techniques for improving, 62
  "three I" approach to, 49–53
  through storytelling, 54–56
  transparency and honesty in, 59
  of vision, 5
  with your boss, 6–7
  (*See also* Performance conversations)
Communication gap, 45–46, 49
Communication model, 44
Company culture, 8, 17, 233
Company policies, negative talk about,
  140–141
  (*See also* Policy violation problems)
Competence, in learning model, 33
Compliance, documenting problems for, 119
Conduct problems (*see* Behavior and conduct
  problems)
Conflict between employees, 125–126
Consciousness, in learning model, 33
Consistency, in documenting problems,
  118–119
Context, in communications, 60, 61
Continuous improvement, 209
Conversational communication, 57
Corrective feedback, in four-step model,
  30–31
Culture:
  company (*see* Company culture)
  performance, 233–235
Customer service, substandard, 84–85,
  127–128

Deadlines, missing, 126
Defensiveness, 23
deGersdorff, Myra, 40–41
Delegation, 110–114
Deming, W. Edwards, 207
Departments:
  alignment of, 40–47
  interdepartmental communications, 7
Diagnostic tool kit, 204–207
Discussion template, 33–36
Disorganized workstation problem, 139–140
Documentation, 118–120, 217
Documents, updating, 6
Dole, Bob, 57
*Don't Throw Underwear on the Table &
  Other Lessons Learned at Work* (Scott
  Carbonara), 63
Drama in the workplace (*see* Workplace
  drama)

Dress code violations, 88–89, 133
"Drive-by" feedback, 18
Driver style, 115, 117
Drucker, Peter, 220
Dynamics of workplace, 155–168
  drama, 155–163
  long-distance employees, 166–168
  multiple generations, 163–165

"Early wins," 10, 15
eBay, 58
Edison, Thomas, 56
E-mail misuse, 90–91, 128–129
Emerson, Ralph Waldo, 230
Emotional management, 162
Employee Coaching and Development Plan,
  170–201
  performance improvement steps in, 170–173
  templates for, 174–201
Employees:
  alignment of, 40–47
  conflict between, 125–126
  encouraging participation of, 123
  expecting the best from, 226
  feedback from, 64
  four-step model role of, 23–26
  long-distance, 166–168
  maintaining self-esteem of, 123
  motivating, 114–118
  multiple generations of, 163–165
  (*See also* New employees)
Empowerment, for delegated assignments,
  113–114
Energy, mastery of, 161–162
Error rates, unacceptable, 86–87, 127
Excessive absences, 102–103, 129–130
Excessive tardiness, 100–101
Expectations, 1–19
  based on strategic vision, 2–5
  clarity of, 29
  communication of, 5–8
  and company culture, 8
  for delegated assignments, 113
  in four-step model, 29–30
  during onboarding process, 9–19
  in Performance Builder, 216
  for team, 4–5
Expense irregularities, 98–99, 134–135
Experiential follow-up assignment, 223, 225

Facts:
  providing context for, 60, 61
  stories vs., 54, 56

Family Medical Leave Act (FMLA) abuse, 104–105
Feedback:
  on communications, 63, 64
  corrective, 30–31
  during onboarding, 15–19
  in Performance Builder, 218–219
  on small stuff, 34
  "soft sandwich" approach to, 170
  for younger generations of employees, 17–18
Figures:
  in performance rankings, 210
  stories vs., 54, 56
Firsthand Lessons, Secondhand Dogs (Scott Carbonara), 62
FMLA (Family Medical Leave Act) abuse, 104–105
Follow-through, lack of, 82–83, 132–133
Follow-up:
  lack of, 82–83
  in Performance Builder, 217
Four-step performance management model, 21–37
  assess step in, 27–28
  coach and correct step in, 30–31
  measure results step in, 32
  performance conversations based on, 33–36
  for performance success, 67
    (*See also* Performance success)
  roles and responsibilities in, 22–26
  set expectations step in, 29–30

Gallup, 43
Gap analysis, 232, 233
Gap management, 158
Gen Xers, 164, 165
Gen Yers, 164, 165
General Electric (GE), 56
Generations of employees, 163–165
Goethe, Johann Wolfgang von, 151
Gossip, spreading, 72–73, 137–138

Habits, annoying, 142–143
Hampel, Brenda, 234–235
Harassment, 180–181, 186–187, 237–239
High-intensity listening, 62, 63
Hiring manager, in onboarding process, 11, 12
Honesty, 59, 159
Hsieh, Tony, 57

Human resources (HR) partner:
  company culture information from, 8
  documentation review by, 120
  four-step model role of, 22–26
  in onboarding process, 11
HumanResourcesSources.org, 169, 173
Humorous feedback, 19
Hygiene, unacceptable, 96–97, 136

I Love Lucy video clip, 203–204
IBM, 220
IKEA, 61
Inappropriate conversations with coworkers, 135
Inappropriate language, 68–69, 130–131
Inappropriate use of technology, 92–93
Independent style, 117
Influence, in "three I" approach, 50
Information:
  for assessment of work, 27–28
  openness of, 59
  in "three I" approach, 49, 50
Inspiration, in "three I" approach, 49, 50
Integration plan, 10
  (*See also* Onboarding)
Intel, 53
Intentional communication, 61
Interdepartmental communications, 7
Interrupting, problem with, 150–151

JetBlue Airways Corporation, 213–214
Job abandonment, 94–95, 137
Job requirements, not meeting, 70–71

Karpman drama triangle, 160, 161
Keeping leader informed, problems with, 138–139
Kelleher, Herb, 55
King, Martin Luther, Jr., 58
Knowledge, as onboarding objective, 15

Lack of understanding, starters for conversations about, 146–147
Language:
  as cultural barrier, 243–244
  inappropriate, 68–69, 130–131
Leaders:
  assessment of situation by, 27–28
  "brand" of, 37
  coaching and correction by, 30–31
  communication errors of, 51–53
  expectations set by, 29

Leaders *(continued)*:
  four-step model role of, 22, 24–26
  proactive, 107
"Leadership brand," 37
Leadership problems, 80–81, 151–154
Learning model, 33
Listening:
  active, 45–47
  high-intensity, 62, 63
  in order to motivate, 124
  problems with, 150–151
London Business School, 211–212
Long-distance performance management,
    166–168

Management style case study, 241–242
Maslow's hierarchy of needs, 245
MBTI (Myers-Briggs Type Indicator), 115
Measuring results:
  of communication, 52–53
  in four-step model, 32
  (See also Performance measurement)
Meetings:
  during onboarding, 16
  with team, 6
  unpreparedness for, 149–150
  with your boss, 7
Messy workstation problems, 139–140
Microsoft, 64
Minimum job requirements, not meeting,
    70–71
Missing deadlines, 126
Montanez, Stephanie, 169–173, 235
Motivation, 114–118, 124
Multigenerational workplace, 163–165
Myers-Briggs Type Indicator (MBTI), 115

Needs, hierarchy of, 245
Negativity:
  about company policies, 140–141
  and workplace drama, 159
New employees:
  conversation starters for managing,
    124–125
  feedback for, 16–19
  onboarding plan for, 9–16
90-day mailback worksheet, 223, 224
90-day plan, 10
  (See also Onboarding)
Nonverbal communication, 152–154
Nordstrom, 46
Noyce, Robert, 53

Onboarding, 9–19
  developing plan for, 9–16
  feedback during, 16–19
  key objectives in, 14–16
  managing plan for, 16
  and performance management, 233,
    234
  roles and responsibilities in, 10–12
  sample plan for, 13–14
  "three-legged stool" model of, 10–11
Out of Crisis (W. Edwards Deming), 207
Overall performance problems, 131–132

Peale, Norman Vincent, 159
People skills, lack of, 239–240
Performance Builder, 215–226
Performance conversations:
  balance in, 23–26
  at best-in-class organizations, xiv–xv, 21
  guidelines for, 123–124
  practicing, 34
  reasons for not having, xiii
  starters for *(see* Starters for performance
    conversations)
  template for, 33–36
Performance culture, 233–235
Performance feedback, onboarding feedback
    vs., 17
Performance improvement:
  requirements for, 238
  steps in, 170–173
    (See also Employee Coaching and
      Development Plan)
  using strategies for, 235–244
  whole-person approach to, 229–235
Performance measurement, 203–228
  art of, 226
  case studies of, 210–214
  diagnostic tool kit for, 204–207
  discussion starters about, 228
  effectiveness of, 214–215, 227–228
  goal of, 209
  leader's checklist for, 227
  Performance Builder tool for, 215–226
  and performance reviews, 208–209
  reevaluating current tools for, 207
  for team members, 228
Performance problems:
  attendance and tardiness, 100–105
  behavior and conduct, 68–77
  case studies of, 235–244
  diagnostic tool kit for, 204–207

with overall performance, 131–132
    policy violations, 88–99
    preventing (*see* Preventing performance
        problems)
    steps in handling, 173
    work performance, 78–87
    (*See also specific types of problems*)
Performance reviews, 208–209
Performance success, 67–105
    Attendance and Tardiness worksheets and
        templates, 100–105
    Behavior and Conduct Problems
        worksheets and templates, 68–77
    and onboarding objectives, 15–16
    Policy Violation worksheets and templates,
        88–99
    Work Performance worksheets and
        templates, 78–87
Persecutors, 160–161
Personal development scorecard, 220–222
Personal hygiene, unacceptable, 96–97, 136
Personal life issues, 229–230
Personal phone calls, 143–144, 194–195
    (*See also* Cell phone policy)
Pixar, 62
Policy violation problems, 88–99
    case study of, 237–239
    cell phone policy, 182–185, 188–189,
        192–193
    company dress code, 88–89, 133
    e-mail misuse, 90–91, 128–129
    harassment, 180–181, 186–187, 237–239
    inappropriate use of technology, 92–93
    job abandonment, 94–95
    personal phone calls, 143–144, 194–195
    safety policies, 141–142, 190–191
    social networking misuse, 194–195
    timekeeping, 196–197
    travel expense irregularities, 98–99,
        134–135
    unacceptable personal hygiene, 96–97, 136
    under the influence at work, 76–77,
        148–149
Politically incorrect behavior, 74–75
"Praise in progress," 209
Preventing performance problems:
    at best-in-class organizations, 40
    feedback for, 16–19, 63, 64
    with proactive communication, 47–49
    steps in, 54–64
Prioritizing responsibilities, 109
Proactive communication, 47–49

Proactive performance management,
    107–120
    coaching in, 108–109
    delegation in, 110–114
    documentation in, 118–120
    motivation in, 114–118
    plan for, 107, 109
    and workplace drama, 163
Procedures, not following, 144
Processes, resistance to changes in, 147–148
Protection, documenting problems for, 119

Q12 research (Gallup), 43
Qualex, 169
Quelch, John A., 211
"Quick hits," 10

Realignment, in managing workplace drama,
    159–160
Recognition and control style, 117
Reinvention, in managing workplace drama,
    159–160
Relationship development, 10, 15–16, 43
Relationship drama, 160–161
Relationship style, 117
Repetition, in communication, 58–59
Rescuers, 160–161
Resistance:
    to a change in processes, 147–148
    releasing, 162
Responsibilities (*see* Roles and
    responsibilities)
Results, measuring, 32, 52–53
    (*See also* Performance measurement)
Return on investment (ROI), 226
Ritz-Carlton Hotels, 40–41, 109
Roles and responsibilities:
    in four-step performance management
        model, 22–26
    in onboarding process, 10–12
Rules, enforcing, 158
Rumors, spreading, 72–73, 137–138

Safety violations, 141–142, 190–191
Secondhand feedback, 19
Secretiveness, 59
Secure and stable style, 117
Self-esteem, maintaining, 123
Setbacks, reinventing and realigning after,
    159–160
Sexual harassment policy violation, 237–239
60-second rule, 154

SMART objectives, 29–30

Social networking misuse, 194–195

"Soft sandwich" approach, 170

"Speedback," 218–219

Staff meetings, 6

Starters for performance conversations,
    121–154
    on angry outbursts, 145
    on being under the influence at work,
        148–149
    on coming to meetings unprepared,
        149–150
    on company dress code violations, 133
    on conflict between employees, 125–126
    on e-mail misuse, 128–129
    on excessive absences, 129–130
    on frequent absence from work area, 146
    on habits that are annoying to others,
        142–143
    on inappropriate language, 130–131
    on job abandonment, 137
    on lack of follow-through, 132–133
    on leadership performance challenges,
        151–154
    on messy/disorganized workstation,
        139–140
    on missing deadlines, 126
    on negative talk about company policies,
        140–141
    on not keeping your leader informed,
        138–139
    on overall performance, 131–132
    on regularly interrupting/not listening,
        150–151
    on repeatedly not following procedures,
        144
    on resistance to change of a process,
        147–148
    on safety violations, 141–142
    on saying "I understand" without really
        understanding, 146–147
    on spreading gossip and rumors, 137–138
    on substandard customer service, 127–128
    on talking inappropriately to coworkers,
        135
    on too many personal phone calls,
        143–144
    on travel expense irregularities, 134–135
    on unacceptable error rates, 127
    on unacceptable personal hygiene, 136
    when managing new employees, 124–125

Stop Workplace Drama (Marlene Chism), 156

Storytelling, 54–56

Substandard customer service, 84–85,
    127–128

Suitor, Vicki, 159

Sun Microsystems Inc., 212–213

Synchronicity, 40–47

Talent management cycle, xv–xvi

Talking inappropriately to coworkers:
    inappropriate language, 68–69, 130–131
    starters for conversations about, 135

Tardiness, excessive, 100–101

Target Corporation, 63

Team members:
    assessing, 111–114
    measuring performance of, 228

Teams:
    communication with, 6–7
    creating, 1–2
    vision for, 2–5

Teamwork, lack of, 78–79

Technology, inappropriate use of, 92–93

Templates:
    Attendance and Tardiness Problems, 101,
        103, 105
    Behavior and Conduct Problems, 69, 71,
        73, 75, 77
    Employee Coaching and Development
        Plan, 174–201
    experiential follow-up assignment, 225
    Motivating Others, 115, 116
    90-day mailback worksheet, 224
    for performance conversations, 33–36
    personal development scorecard, 221–222
    Policy Violation Problems, 89, 91, 93, 95,
        97, 99
    "Speedback," 219
    Team Assessment, 112
    Work Performance Problems, 79, 81, 83,
        85, 87

"Three I" communication, 49–53

"Three-legged stool" onboarding model,
    10–11

Timekeeping policy violations, 196–197

Time-based check-ins, 46–47

Traditionalists, 164, 165

Training:
    importance of, 220
    of new employees, 9–19
    for performance improvement, 171–172

Transition plan, 10
  (*See also* Onboarding)
Transparency, in communication, 59
Travel expense irregularities, 98–99, 134–135

Unacceptable error rates, 86–87, 127
Unacceptable personal hygiene, 96–97, 136
Under the influence at work, 76–77, 148–149
Understanding, not admitting lack of, 146–147
Unpreparedness for meetings, 149–150

Victims, 160–161
Virgin Group, 48
Vision, 2–5

Welch, Jack, 56
"We-opic" vision, 2
Whole Foods, 51
Whole-person approach, 229–235
Winfrey, Oprah, 55
Work area, absence from, 146
Work outcomes, establishing (*see* Expectations)
Work performance problems, 78–87
  frequent absence from work area, 146
  inappropriate use of technology, 92–93
  lack of follow-up and follow-through, 82–83, 132–133
  lack of people skills, 239–240
  lack of teamwork, 78–79
  leadership problems, 80–81, 151–154
  missing deadlines, 126

not admitting lack of understanding, 146–147
not following procedures, 144
not keeping leader informed, 138–139
not meeting minimum job requirements, 70–71
resistance to changes in processes, 147–148
substandard customer service, 84–85, 127–128
unacceptable error rates, 86–87, 127
unpreparedness for meetings, 149–150
workstation messiness/disorganization, 139–140
Workplace drama, 155–163
  and clarity, 156–157
  creative management of, 162–163
  and gap management, 158
  and mastery of energy, 161–162
  and reinvention/realignment, 159–160
  relationship drama, 160–161
  and resistance, 162
  and telling the truth, 159
Worksheets:
  Attendance and Tardiness, 100, 102, 104
  Behavior and Conduct, 68, 70, 72, 74, 76
  Policy Violation, 88, 90, 92, 94, 96, 98
  Work Performance, 78, 80, 82, 84, 86
Workstation, messy and disorganized, 139–140

Zappos, 57

About the Authors

Anne Bruce dispenses humor, wisdom, wit, and practical insights taken from her worldwide travels and life-altering adventures, both in her books and from the speaker's platform and the international seminar stage. She has built a global reputation as a disarming and impactful human behaviorist and entertaining speaker on employee motivation. She also brings her skills and knowledge to building workplace morale, global leadership, and improving performance in the workplace. She's the bestselling author of more than 16 books—and still counting—and a busy employee development coach.

Anne can't speak enough, or write enough, about the power of passionate people, igniting human potential, and growing and branding extraordinary talent. Nor can she say enough about the unflappable attitudes that inspire and align organizations and their people to levels of success they never dreamed possible. As a successful author, Anne's consistent and powerful message teaches audiences that our thoughts and words all take part in shaping the future.

Anne has had the privilege to speak, write, or train for prestigious organizations, such as the White House, the Pentagon, Sony International, Accenture, Best Buy, Coca-Cola, GEICO, Southwest Airlines, Harvard and Stanford Law Schools, Sprint, the Conference Board of Europe, Ben & Jerry's, JetBlue, Baylor University Medical Center, the Southern Company, the American Society of Training and Development (ASTD), the Ritz-Carlton Hotels, the Social Security Administration, and the American Red Cross.

Her books have been translated into more than 24 languages worldwide, and include works published on both personal and professional development, including: *Speak for a Living: The Insider's Guide to Building a Speaking Career* (ASTD Press), *Discover True North: A 4-Week Approach to Ignite Your Passion and Activate Your Potential* (McGraw-Hill), *Be Your Own Mentor* (McGraw-Hill), *Motivating Employees* (McGraw-Hill), *Building a High Morale Workplace* (McGraw-Hill), *How to Motivate Every Employee* (McGraw-Hill), *Leaders—Start to Finish: A Roadmap for Training and Developing Leaders at All Levels* (ASTD Press), *Perfect Phrases for Documenting Employee Performance Problems* (McGraw-Hill), and *Perfect Phrases for Employee Development Plans* (McGraw-Hill).

Anne has appeared on the *CBS Evening News, Today Show* segments, and as a guest on the *Charlie Rose Show.* She's worked extensively in broadcast journalism and has contributed interviews to *Good Morning America* and NBC, journalism and has contributed interviews to *Good Morning America* and NBC, MSNBC, ABC, FOX, and CNN news programs. She's been written about in distinguished print media, including *USA Today, The Times* (London), *The Wall Street Journal,* the *San Jose Mercury News,* and numerous magazines, including *Newsweek.*

Anne and her husband David enjoy the beach life in the greater Los Angeles area where Anne is currently writing and developing a series of novels and a screenplay.

For information on keynote speeches, workshops, and training programs associated with this book and others, visit Anne's Web site at www. AnneBruce.com. For details on how you can bring this book's training program on *Solving Employee Performance Problems* to your organization; additional leadership seminars; keynotes; and training workshops; or for fees, availability, and to schedule press interviews, please call 214-507-8242, or e-mail Anne@AnneBruce.com, for more information.

Brenda Hampel and **Erika Lamont** have consulted, coached, inspired, and developed operational and human resources teams to create onboarding and leadership development experiences at TJX Companies, Cardinal Health, Audi of America, Volkswagen Group of America, Chico's FAS, Sara Lee Food and Beverage, The Ohio State University Medical Center, Coach Inc., DSW, Victoria's Secret, and NCR/Teradata.

Brenda and Erika are contributing authors to *Creating Effective Onboarding Programs* by Doris S. Sims (McGraw-Hill, 2010). They are also quoted leadership onboarding experts in the following articles: "Obama's Onboarding Offers Lessons," SHRM online (February 2009); "Diving In," Susan Wells, *Society for Human Resource Magazine* (2005); and "Execs On Board," Ed Silverman, *Human Resource Executive Magazine* (2003).

Brenda Hampel is a founding partner with Connect the Dots Consulting. She works with executive teams and team leaders to help them understand how to leverage their individual and combined strengths to create strategies for addressing gaps that prevent the leaders from achieving their business objectives. In addition to her consulting experience with executives in Fortune 50 companies, Brenda has held human resources leadership roles at ABB; Bath and Body Works, a division of Limited Brands; and Cardinal Health.

Brenda graduated from The Ohio State University with a BA in communications and has continued her education by participating in executive programs (human resources curriculum) at the University of Michigan and The Ohio State University.

Brenda has been invited to present at numerous professional conferences including, SHRM HR Southwest, The HR Technology Show, IQPC Onboarding Talent, and CAI HR Management.

Erika Lamont is also a partner at Connect the Dots Consulting and has worked with clients to create solutions for leadership onboarding, individual leadership coaching, alignment for mergers and acquisitions, as well as team and individual skills assessment and action planning. Erika has also held leadership roles inside large organizations such as Riverside Methodist Hospital, part of the OhioHealth Corporation and Bath & Body Works, a division of Limited Brands.

Erika brings a distinctive blend of operational experience and leadership development skills to her client base. She earned a BA degree in political science from Miami University in Oxford, Ohio, and has received extensive professional development in leadership coaching, managing teams, total quality management, supply chain development, and project management.

She has been a presenter for national conferences in human resources, such as SHRM HR Southwest, HR Tech, and IQPC Onboarding Talent, as well as hospital association conferences and professional procurement organizations.

Both Brenda Hampel and Erika Lamont are available to present workshops and presentations on effectively managing employee performance. They also provide consulting in the areas of team dynamics, leadership development, and coaching. Please contact them at 1-877-793-8805 or bhampel@connectthedotsconsulting.com or elamont@connect thedotsconsulting.com.